STEP by STEP
BASKETBALL
SKILLS

Joe Whelton

Edited by
Richard Taylor

Specially commissioned
photographs by
Neil Robinson

HAMLYN

Acknowledgements

Front cover: All-Sport (UK)/Brian Drake
All photographs by Neil Robinson/International Sports Book Network
except the following
All-Sport (UK) 7 top, Brian Drake 25, 41, 91, 99, Mike Powell 75, 88;
All-Sport (USA) Tony Duffy 9, 29, Mike Powell 10, 38, 63, 90, 120;
Steven A. Roseboro 47, 64, 78, 123

Artwork   Mei Lim

The author and publisher would like to thank Mike Burton, Dave Gardner,
Cliff Jones, Jason Fogerty, Peter Mullings and Curtis Hunter

Published by
The Hamlyn Publishing Group Limited
a division of The Octopus Group plc
Michelin House, 81 Fulham Road
London SW3 6RB
and distributed for them by
Octopus Distribution Services Limited
Rushden, Northamptonshire NN10 9RZ

First published in 1988

ISBN 0 600 50349 6

Printed in Spain by Graficromo, S. A.- Córdoba

KEY TO DIAGRAMS
Figures in white vests represent offensive players
Figures in black vests represent defensive players

──────▶	running
─────┤	running to block path
┈┈┈┈▶	passing
⋙⋙▶	dribbling
C	coach

CONTENTS

Foreword 6
About the author and editor 7
Introduction 8
Dribbling 10
Passing 18
Shooting 26
Rebounding 40
Man-to-man defence 50
Zone defence 62
Individual moves 74
Man-to-man offence 90
Work-outs 104
Training and practice 112
Basketball assessment test 118
Running the game 120
Referee's signals 122
Glossary 124
Addresses 126
Index 127

FOREWORD

**BY THE SECRETARY OF THE
ENGLISH BASKET BALL
ASSOCIATION**

In 1991 basketball will be celebrating the centenary of the invention of the game. Originally conceived as a gymnasium game for use by the students at the YMCA Training College at Springfield, Massachusetts, USA, it has now progressed to become one of the most extensively played sports in the world.

Basketball requires skill, dexterity, agility, alertness, co-ordination and the ability of individual players to co-operate to form a team.

Joe Whelton, coach to the Great Britain Olympic team in 1988 has written a book which we are pleased to endorse and recommend to both players and club coaches. The book covers the basic individual and team skills and develops these into the game situation. It offers an excellent source of technical information for both players and coaches and will certainly help teams to win matches in the future.

Mel Welch
Secretary
English Basket Ball Association
Leeds, England

ABOUT THE AUTHOR AND EDITOR

Joe Whelton completed his basketball career in the United States then rapidly built a reputation as one of Europe's rising young coaches with the famous name of Manchester United. Whelton was named England's Coach of the Year in 1985 then went on to coach the Great Britain team in the 1988 Olympic programme in a tournament alongside the former Olympic and World Champions the Soviet Union, former Olympic Champions Yugoslavia and former Olympic finalists, Spain and Italy.

Joe Whelton was born in Hartford, Connecticut, in 1956, and his basketball career began at the local East Catholic High School. His outstanding high school career led to many offers of scholarships from major colleges before he decided to stay at the local University of Connecticut, where he graduated in special education.

Whelton's career in English basketball began in 1983 and at the end of that season his Manchester United team reached the Championship Final at the world-famous Wembley Arena. The following season the team won the Championship Final and then in 1986 won the National League with a run of 20 consecutive victories. Whelton has also been heavily involved in coaching and teaching at clinics for aspiring young players in one of England's fastest-developing sports.

Joe and his wife Patty have two daughters, Jamie and Jessica.

Richard Taylor is the only freelance journalist in the United Kingdom specializing in basketball and writes columns for *The Daily Telegraph* and *The Independent* national newspapers as well as for the *London Evening Standard*, where he was on the staff from 1971 until 1978. When he became a freelance in 1978 he was appointed editor of *Basketball Monthly*, the United Kingdom's premier basketball magazine. Working for the magazine and newspapers he has covered basketball in the United States, the Soviet Union, several other countries in Eastern Europe and all the basketball-playing nations of Western Europe as well as Greece and Turkey. Richard Taylor and his wife Dr Joan Taylor live in Leicestershire with their daughters Meredith and Greer and their son Richard.

INTRODUCTION

When Dr James Naismith devised a game to keep his college students quiet, he could never have guessed it would keep the world's sportsmen and sportswomen busy for the next hundred years.

In 1891 Dr Naismith was a PE instructor in Springfield in the American state of Massachusetts and during a harsh winter tried to give his students an indoor alternative to gymnastics. He drew up 13 basic rules and put them to the test in January 1892 in a game which had its emphasis on skill with the hands, rather than the feet. Players could not run with the ball in their hands, but they could bounce it, and the target was a demanding one – a basket nailed to the balconies at each end of the gymnasium, well above head height.

Those baskets have been the target for millions of basketball players ever since and it is the players and their coaches who are at the heart of the game.

The coach has far more influence in basketball *during matches* than is the case in most other team sports. When the game is going away from his team he can call a time-out to stop play, change his tactics and hope for an immediate change of fortune.

Some coaches say there are two basic rules to the game:

Rule 1: The coach is always right

Rule 2: When the coach is wrong . . . see Rule 1

Well, maybe that is over-stating the case a little, but it is true to say that a team's style of play results from the philosophy of its coach and he or she must epitomize all the qualities that they want to see in their players. The coach is a teacher on and off the court and that applies for school and youth club players just as much as for senior teams. That is why a book such as this is so important. It does not just tell you how to play, but also brings an insight into the way a coach thinks and underlines those qualities he or she will look for in their players.

Olympic Games, World Championships, Continental Championships for national teams and dozens of international competitions for club teams are underpinned by the countless local and national leagues for men, women and children which have made basketball one of the world's most popular team sports.

In the park or the playground . . . hustling with your friends in the school gym during lunch break . . . playing for your country or even in a national league for a men's, women's or junior team: whichever level you play basketball at now there are always new targets to aim for, higher standards to reach.

Basketball can satisfy all the challenges sport has to offer, both as an individual and as a member of a team. Striving to reach all those demanding, personal goals will make you a better player, in a better team and it is my goal in this book to help you achieve those aims. Most importantly I hope I will help you to develop as a player so you can make your team into a stronger side. Remember, basketball is a *team* game and much of the excitement comes from blending individual talents into a smooth and powerful sporting machine.

Your starting point is a simple desire – the desire to play. Back home in Hartford, Connecticut, in my teens I planned my out-of-school hours around where I could pick up the best game in a local park or playground. These 'pick up' games were a major part of my life. On a Monday evening I would be off to one particular playground because I knew that was where the toughest kids would be getting together. On Tuesdays I would make my way to a different part of the city where the locals had a game that night, and so it would go on.

I'll always remember Thursday nights because that was when the best 'pick up' game was played five miles away from our house, across the other side of Hartford. The distance didn't stop me though, it provided an opportunity to keep up my fitness getting there – and returning home after the game!

I know England doesn't yet offer the same opportunities for outside basketball. But if you have the determination to improve your game there is no shortage of routes to reaching the top, on your own, with two or three friends or under the guidance of a teacher or youth leader. My drills and practice schedules, charts and checklists will enable you to keep a track of your progress.

Believe me, basketball can be so much more than just a game to you. While you develop your skills, basketball will help you to develop your personality on and off the court. Always strive to do your best, be the best and be ready to rise to the thrill of competition.

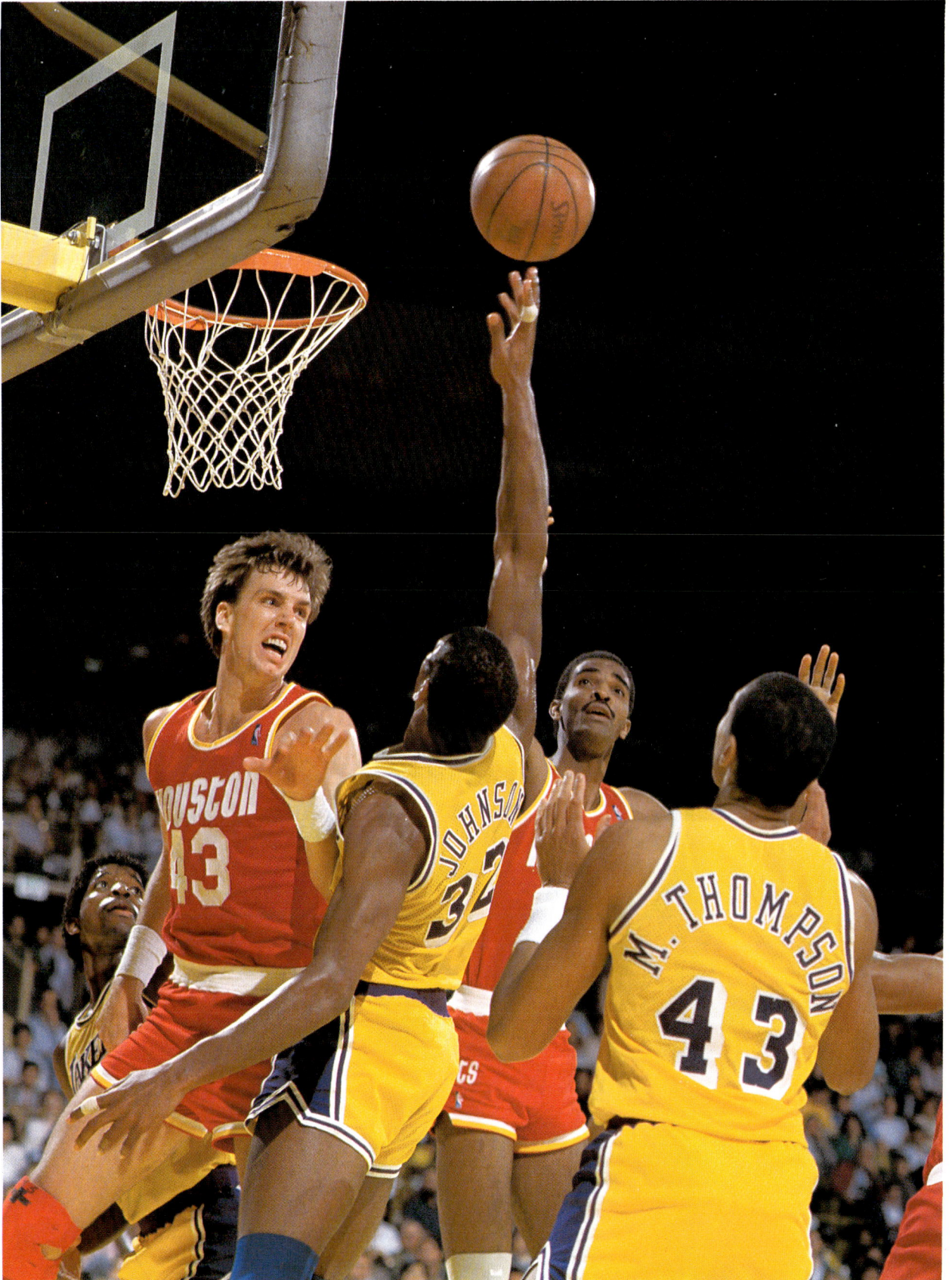

DRIBBLING

The lowest of low dribbles from Isiah Thomas of the Detroit Pistons as he prepares to make his move past a defender

I know, it looks exciting. The player with the ball darts in and out of defenders like a slalom skier and they may as well try to catch a shadow as stop him. Well, this is where I'm going to surprise a lot of you. If that's your idea of dribbling, you're mistaken. Dribbling the basketball is the most misused skill any young player can master.

When you watch the best basketball teams in the world play, you soon realize that dribbling is used only as a weapon on offence, what we call attack. Watch American professional teams like the Boston Celtics of the National Basketball Association (NBA), or one of the international teams playing in an Olympic Games. No team at any level, either international, professional or even in local or schools' basketball can find an offensive rhythm when a player or players are dominating possession with excessive dribbling of the ball. Less dribbling makes better basketball!

Dribbling should be used only in particular situations on court. For example, to free a player from a defensive trap; when a dribbler can put himself in a better position to shoot the ball; to create a clear driving lane to the basket and to create an opportunity for a better placed team-mate.

If you're going to dribble, do it the right way. First of all the dribbler must keep his head up, looking for opportunities to open up an offence. A dribbler must be able to see an 'open' team-mate, one who is free from a defender in front of him. If a team-mate is available for a pass, the player with the ball should not be dribbling, but passing! Dribble the ball only when it is a positive move for yourself or a team-mate.

Like any other skill in basketball, dribbling can be improved only through constant individual practice. There is little use in arriving for practice and dribbling the ball for a few minutes. Take the ball wherever you go. If you walk to practice at school or at a playground, don't carry the ball, dribble it!

Dribble halfway with your right hand and halfway with your left. This is vital, because no-one can play basketball using only one hand. If you're right-handed you should practise dribbling twice as long with your left hand. If you are left-handed put in the extra work with your right.

ISIAH THOMAS

★Isiah Lord Thomas III was born in Chicago, Illinois, in 1961. He went to Westchester High School and then on to Indiana University at Bloomington. He was selected to play in the NBA by the Detroit Pistons at the end of his undergraduate year in 1981 after winning the US College Championship with Indiana. Thomas held the NBA record for the most assists in one season – 1,123.

Protected or controlled dribble

Now, let's apply ball-handling skills to competition. Once you've gained better control of the ball, it's time to put a defensive player into the picture. You have the ball, the defender wants it, so you must know how to protect the ball. At all times while being defended closely, you should keep your body between the ball and the defender. Have your knees bent, your body low and your free arm bent at the elbow but parallel to the floor as a shield against the defender while keeping the ball bouncing as close to the floor as possible. Having the knees bent and the body crouching low helps to hide the ball from the defender while your free arm can be used as a buffer between you.

The ball must be kept in a low bounce so that you don't 'show the ball'; to practise this skill try a slow and controlled dribble, concentrating on maintaining position in protecting the ball.

Keep your body between the ball and the defender, knees bent, body low and free arm used as a shield

Speed dribble

The speed dribble is used when you want to push the ball down the floor quickly as in the type of move we call a 'fast break', when the defending team gain possession and move swiftly out of defence into counter-attack. The dribbler runs fast, but always under control, pushing the ball 3 to 4 ft (1 m) out in front of him with the ball coming up to about waist height at the end of the bounce. You must keep your head up with your eyes looking ahead to spot an open team-mate who could receive a pass from you.

Speed dribble practice
Start at one endline or baseline of the basketball court and push the ball out in front of you using a speed dribble. Go all the way down court to the far baseline and then stop or make a pass against the wall before turning and repeating the sprint back up the floor, this time using your opposite hand to dribble.

Repeat this drill until you can execute the speed dribble without any slips as fast as possible up and down the floor. As well as practising the speed dribble this is also good for conditioning and will simulate game conditions by forcing you to dribble as you become more and more tired.

1 Push the ball 3 ft (1 m) to 4 ft (1.3 m) out in front, while running fast but under control

2 Make sure the ball comes up to waist height

1

2

WHELTON'S TIPS

● *Too much dribbling destroys a team's rhythm. Less dribbling makes for better basketball*

> ❛ Keep the ball low to the floor, then explode past the defender towards the basket ❜

1 When you're dribbling bounce the ball from left hand to right

2 With the ball in your right hand step across the defender putting your body between the defender and the ball

Crossover dribble
3-5 Keep your body low, the bounce low and crossover the ball between hands with every step

Crossover dribble

This is used to move around and then past a defender. While dribbling with your right hand, as you approach the defender you dribble one low bounce crossing the ball to your left hand and step around the defender. This puts the lead leg and your body between the defender and the ball. The crossover dribble obviously can be used left to right as well as right to left. It is very important that the crossover dribble is kept low to the floor as you explode past the defender towards the basket.

Crossover dribble practice
Walk up and down the court with your knees bent, body low, dribbling while crossing the ball from hand to hand with every step. Walk forwards and backwards, keeping the dribble as low as possible, always with your eyes looking straight in front of you with your head up.

Spin dribble

This is ideal for protecting the ball. With the ball in your right hand and your body protecting it, you pivot on your left foot and bring the ball waist high and spin yourself with your back to the defender. Take one large step with your right foot as you come out of the spin while exchanging the ball to your left hand and then sprint past the defender and towards the basket. The spin dribble takes a lot of practice as you must be careful not to 'carry' the ball, that is have your hand underneath it. This is a violation and will be penalized by the referee. Of course, you must work on spinning left to right as well as right to left.

Spin dribble practice
Start at one endline and imagine defenders are waiting at the nearest free-throw line. Start dribbling hard with your right hand and execute the spin dribble past the imaginary defender and then continue your dribble towards the half-court line, now dribbling with your left hand. Again there is an imaginary defender waiting for you on the half-court line, so you must use the spin dribble again, this time with your left hand to get past the defender. Now you continue down court, this time with your right hand towards the next free-throw line. When you reach it execute the spin dribble again to get past this final defender before the way is open to the basket. Continue up and down the court, spinning with both right and left hands at both free-throw lines and at the half-court line.

CHECK WORDS

Point guard *The ball-handler, play-maker or floor general, excellent passer*
Off guard *Usually taller than the point guard, and a shooter*
Small forward *Often the most athletic team member; can shoot, drive, is fast and a good defender*
Power forward *Tall and strong, a physical player who rebounds and scores close to the basket; the team's 'enforcer'*
Centre *The tallest player, a shot blocker, a rebounder who scores close to the basket; the team's 'intimidator'*
Offence *Individual and team moves which attack your opponents' basket*
Defence *Individual and team moves which defend your basket*
Trap *Two or more defenders trapping the dribbler*
Violation *An offence which loses possession for the team with the ball, but not a personal foul on an opponent*

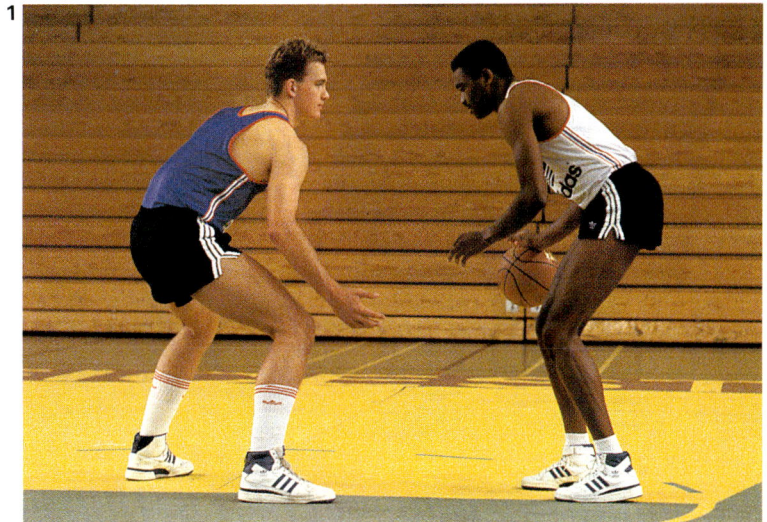
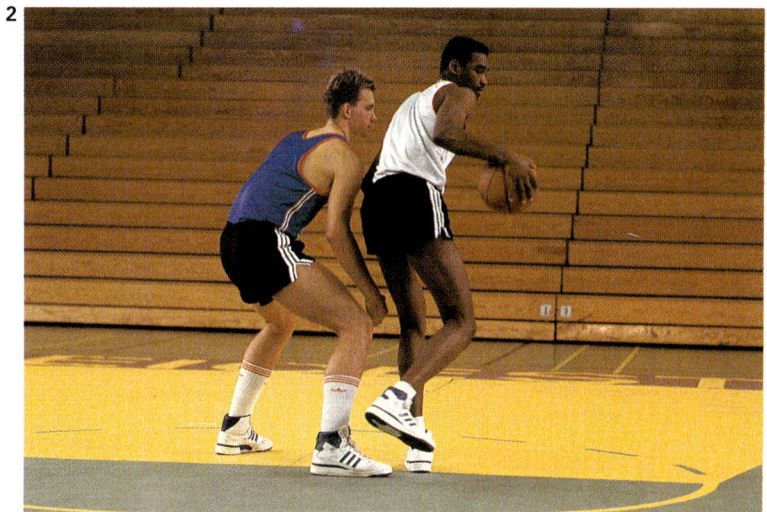
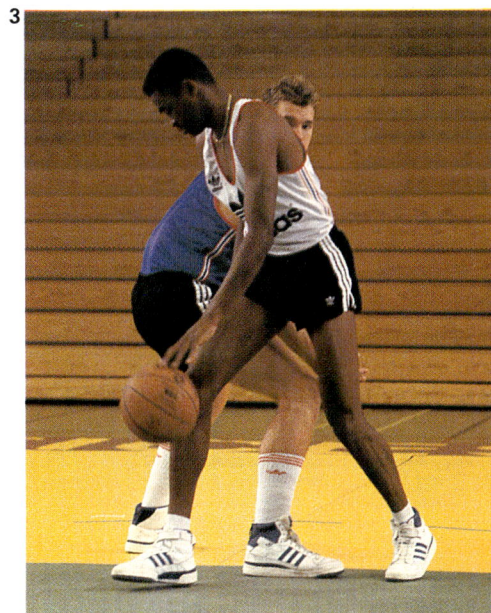

Spin dribble
1 Approach the defender dribbling the ball with your right hand

2 Pivot on your left foot and turn your back on the defender, still dribbling the ball with your right hand

3 Complete the spin, having changed the ball to your left hand and putting your body between the defender and the ball

❝ The shake and bake – an excellent one-on-one move to 'freeze' your defender then leave him standing as you drive for the basket ❞

Stutter step dribble

This is also known as the 'shake and bake' – a phrase derived from the playgrounds of Philadelphia and New York. It is an excellent one-on-one move (when one attacker faces one defender) that 'freezes' a defender. It's a stop-and-go move that's always used when the offensive player is facing the defender.

The dribbler comes towards the defender quickly, then suddenly stutters his feet when within 3 to 4 ft (1 m) of the defensive player. This puts the defender back on his heels, or 'freezes' him. The stutter then becomes an explosive dribble past the defender with your leading leg stepping past your opponent. This move with the leading leg protects the ball as it puts your body between the defender and the ball.

The stutter step is an excellent move to use at the end of the fast break attack, when the team with the ball have switched quickly onto offence trying to catch their opponents before they are organized on defence.

The dribbler leading the fast break can use the stutter step to put his defender, the player guarding him, further off balance. When the player with the ball goes into the stutter step, his defender will probably do one of two things. Either he will straighten up, anticipating that the dribbler is going to attempt a shot. As the defender straightens, ready to block the anticipated shot, the ball-handler now has the ideal opportunity and advantage to dribble past him.

If the stutter step makes the defender drop back on his heels, ready to cover what he expects to be an attempted dribble past him, the ball-handler now has the room to stop and make the jump shot without the defender being close enough to attempt a block.

If the dribbler is being pressured by a defender who is guarding him very closely, he can use the stutter step to change his speed and put the defender off balance. He can then combine the move with a crossover dribble to get past the defender and at the same time put his body between the defender and the ball.

WHELTON'S TIPS

● *Keep your head up, to look for 'open' team-mates and danger from defenders*

● *If a team-mate is open, don't dribble – pass!*

● *Use the between-the-legs dribble only when you're going forward or making room for a shot*

● *If you're moving the ball from your right hand to left, put the left leg forward; from left hand to right, put the right leg forward*

● *Take your ball with you whenever you can, and dribble*

Stutter step dribble
1 Confront the defender with a stutter step

2 Step across the defender with your lead leg, keeping your body between the defender and the ball

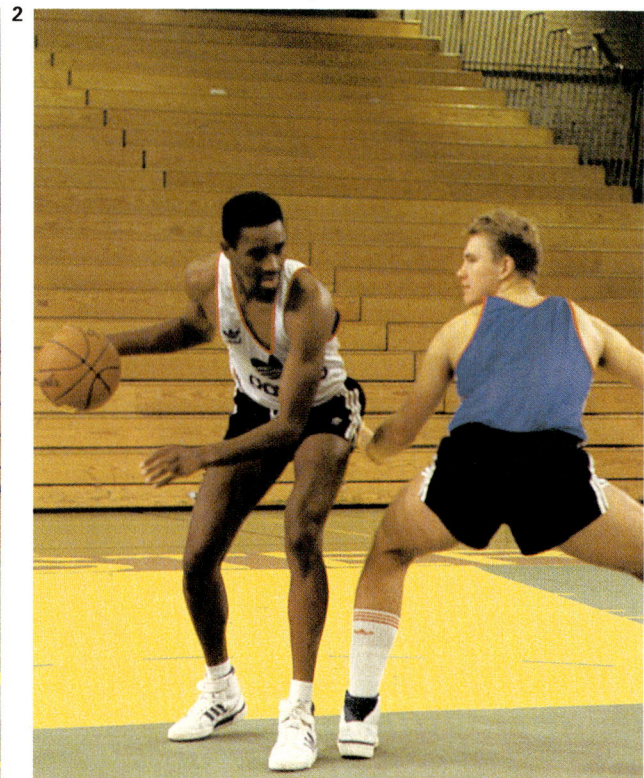

Stutter step dribble practice

Start at the half-court line facing a basket. Dribble towards the hoop with one hand and as you approach the free-throw line imagine that a defender is blocking your way. Use your stutter step 3 to 4 ft (1 m) away from the line and then sprint to the basket as if you were going through to score. Alternate the stutter step move using both your right and left hand. As always, your goal is to be able to use both hands.

Remember, have your head up as you drive past, on the look-out for opportunities and for danger.

Between-the-legs dribble

Coaches used to frown on this and called it 'hot dogging' or showing off. But I think that the between-the-legs dribble can be very effective and advantageous to a player and his team as long as he is doing something positive with the ball and not just trying to impress the crowd.

It's a crossover dribble, in that you change hands, but you do so between the legs. If you want to pass the ball from the right hand to the left you place the left leg forward and the right leg to the rear and bounce the ball between the legs to be collected by the left hand. This is safe, of course, because the ball is protected during the changeover by the leading leg.

The next development in this skill is to be able to bounce the ball between the legs while dribbling and keeping your head up all the time to look out for opponents and team-mates.

As I mentioned, you must know when to use this move. During a game, the between-the-legs dribble is a very effective way of getting past a defender who is pressing against you. Let's say you have the ball in your right hand, so you place your left foot forward and pass the ball between your legs from the right hand to the left.

The defender cannot steal the ball from you because it is protected by your lead leg, and if he makes contact or slaps your leg reaching for the ball he will commit a foul.

Now that you have the ball in your left hand with your left leg across the defender, you can either pull away from him or launch a jump shot.

Remember, use the between-the-legs dribble only when it is part of a positive move towards the basket, otherwise you'll slow down your team's progress up the floor.

Between-the-legs dribble practice

Walk up and down the floor and with every step bounce the ball between your legs from one hand to the other trying not to lose step and not to lose control of the ball. Once you're confident doing this, step up the challenge by continuing the dribble as you return down the floor backwards still bouncing the ball between your legs with every step.

' This is a move to beat opponents – not to impress your friends.

Between-the-legs dribble
1 Put the ball in your right hand and place your left leg forward

2 Play the ball from your right hand to your left through your legs

3 With the ball in your left hand, dribble forwards

' Don't be tempted to look where the ball is. Trust your hands, because if you look down you'll put yourself in danger from an opponent '

Behind-the-back dribble

This is similar to the between-the-legs dribble in that if it is used wisely it can be very effective as well as exciting. It can be used like a spin dribble to keep the ball behind the offensive player and away from the defender, preventing him from reaching to take possession.

When you want to switch the ball from your right hand to the left you must hold the ball around the top, front part, pulling it to the right of your rear. As it reaches that point, change the position of the hand so that the fingers are now on the top rear part of the ball and use them to push it around to the left of your rear into a bounce. After the bounce the ball is gathered in by the left hand which then continues the dribble.

It's vital with this dribble to keep the eyes up and looking ahead. It's a mistake to look down to see where the ball is because by taking your eyes off team-mates and defenders you'll either lose an opportunity to pass or put yourself in danger.

An added advantage of this move is the element of surprise. Few players use the behind-the-back dribble, which makes it more effective if used properly and at the right times.

It's an excellent moment to use this dribble if the defender is guarding you closely and lunges for the ball. Make the behind-the-back dribble and he'll be surprised and off balance, allowing you to sprint away into your dribble with the defender struggling to catch up.

A naturally quick player can use the behind-the-back dribble very effectively, but it also gives an advantage to players who are not naturally quick. Using the behind-the-back dribble can give these players the extra second and extra yard to get away from their defender.

Behind-the-back dribble practice

For this use the same drill as for the spin dribble, pretending there's a defender waiting at each free-throw line and on the half-court line. Implement the skill you learned to keep control of the ball while changing hands at each of these points.

WHELTON'S TIPS

To execute the behind-the-back dribble (moving from the right hand to the left):

● *Pull the ball to your rear by holding the front, top part*

● *Change hand position to hold the top, rear part of the ball*

● *Push the ball to the left hand to continue the dribble*

Behind-the-back dribble
1 Switch the ball from right to left, holding it around the top front part and pulling it to the right of your backside

2 After moving your hand to the top rear part of the ball you can push it to your left hand and continue the dribble

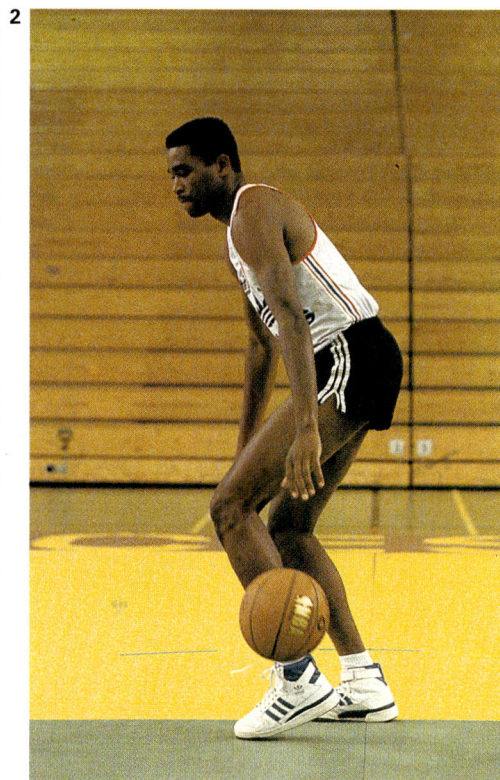

Group drills

Weaving
Place obstacles such as chairs or cones at even spaces on the basketball floor, leaving enough room for the players to weave in and out. Start at one baseline and have a player dribble as quickly as possible, but always with the ball under control, weaving through the obstacles using various dribbles such as the speed, crossover and spin dribble while keeping his head up. They can change from one dribble to another at every obstacle or every other obstacle.

Dribble tag
The entire court can be used for this, but half court will probably be enough. The baselines and sidelines are out of bounds.

All the players dribble with a ball each and at the start of the game the coach names one player as tag or 'it'. That player must try and touch another player while maintaining control over his dribble. A player who is caught becomes 'it'.

Variations to this game include restricting the playing area or allowing the players to dribble with their weak hands only. All the players, of course, must keep control of their balls and steer clear of each other while trying to escape the tag player.

Relay dribble
Break the group up into as many teams as you wish. Each team lines up on the baseline with the first person in each line holding the ball. On the command to start, the players with the balls dribble as fast as they can using the speed dribble. They cross the opposite baseline, turn around and speed dribble back making a two-handed chest pass (page 19) to the next player, who then speed dribbles down the floor.

This is a flexible drill and players can work on other skills by changing the rules. For example, they can use only their weak hands or run crossover dribbles or spin dribbles or whatever they most need to work on.

Command dribble
The players spread out over half the court, each with a ball. Players must dribble in the direction that their coach or teacher points. Therefore they must keep their heads up to watch for the changes in direction. The players will learn to dribble right and left, forwards and backwards and in a stationary position. To ensure that the players are keeping their eyes up, the coach uses the non-directing hand to hold up one, two, three, four or five fingers with the players shouting out the numbers as they change.

Dribble stations
This is the best way to utilize time and space. Split the players into as many groups as you want, say four groups of five players. Each player has a basketball and stands ready with his group at various stations on the floor. On the whistle the first group work on dribbling figure eights (page 107); the second practise the round-the-world dribble (page 107); the third work on the high-low dribble (page 107); the fourth on ball slams (page 105). After two minutes the groups move onto the next station and immediately work on the next skill.

Chair drill
For this drill chairs are ideal obstacles, because they're square and fairly bulky and provide a more difficult manoeuvre for the players. But, if you can't find enough chairs, then cones or waste bins will do.

Make four or five rows of chairs up the court, with each chair between 10 and 15 ft (3 and 5 m) away from the next in its row. The players must dribble in and out of the chairs, keeping their heads up at all times to simulate game conditions when they'll have to be on the look-out for team-mates to receive a pass as well as for opponents who'll want to intercept the passes.

First the players must use a controlled dribble to move in and out of the chairs, being careful not to make contact with the chairs and maintaining control over themselves and the ball at all times. Then they should move onto the speed dribble, while still maintaining control and keeping the head up.

Now simulate game conditions by pretending that the chairs are defenders who have to be beaten by using the variety of dribbles we have discussed in this chapter, to get past the chairs and change direction.

For the first lap of the chairs use the crossover dribble, changing the ball from right to left for the first chair then from left to right for the next chair and so on, repeatedly switching hands at each obstacle until you've completed the lap of chairs back to your starting point. Next, use the behind-the-back dribble, then the between-the-legs and finally the spin dribble.

To introduce that extra edge of competition, get each team to run a relay race against the players in the other lines.

DRIBBLING CHECKLIST

● **Knees bent, body low** *Maintain balance and control while keeping the body between the ball and defender*

● **Protect the ball** *Bend your free arm at the elbow as a buffer between the ball and the defender*

● **Bounce low** *A low bounce stops you 'showing the ball' to the defender*

PASSING

❛ This is the lost art of basketball, because too few players practise passing as readily as they practise shooting and dribbling. But good passing is vital to a team because it creates high percentage shots and brings the players closer together ❜

Introduction

Passing is to me the most exciting aspect of basketball. But it is also the most under-rated skill, which leads me to call it 'the lost art' of basketball.

Around 30 years ago Bob Cousy, who played for the American team Boston Celtics, re-volutionized basketball with his exceptional passing skill. He was nearly always the shortest man on the court, but people bought tickets just to watch him wheel and deal his passes across the floor, leaving his taller opponents baffled and flustered. Cousy's creativity laid the groundwork for future players, with the likes of Isiah Thomas of the Detroit Pistons, Magic Johnson of the Los Angeles Lakers and, of course, the best player in the world today, Larry Bird of the Celtics, thrilling the crowds with their dazzling passes.

Ask any great basketball player what gives him the most satisfaction during the course of the game and nine out of ten will say 'that assist I gave'. Nothing gets a home crowd off their feet quicker than a fast break (page 98) which utilizes great passing and ends with an assist, the name for a great pass which leaves a player open to score with a lay-up (page 32) or a slam dunk (page 36).

Good passing is vital to a team because it sets up good shots from clear positions on the floor from which players have the best chance of scoring. These are called high percentage shots, shots which have the greatest chance of being successful.

Unselfish passing also brings a team closer together more quickly than anything else, and this closeness is necessary to build a winning team. Knowing how and when to pass makes good shooters into great shooters and average shooters a whole lot better!

Before practising the different types of pass remember these rules.
● Passing is the most effective method for moving the ball around the court
● Passing makes the defending team work harder, will tire them and break down their defence to give you the chance to score
● Passing gets everyone involved in the game and underlines the basketball rule that 'the more you give the ball up, the more you will get it back'
● Don't 'telegraph' passes. When possible you should try to look away from your intended

---

BOB COUSY

★*Bob Cousy, one of the all-time great passers of the professional NBA, was born in August 1928 in New York. He wasn't tall for a basketball player, just 6 ft 1 in (1.86 m) which emphasizes how a great passer can control games where some of the players will be a foot taller. Bob Cousy went to high school in New York and then went on to the Holy Cross College in Worcester, Massachusetts, and originally played for an old professional team called the Tri-Cities. But it was when Cousy moved to the Boston Celtics in 1950 that he started on the road to becoming a basketball legend.*

Cousy reached the Championship Play-Offs in every one of the 13 seasons he was with the Celtics and was also voted onto the All-Star Game team in every year. He won Championship titles with the Boston Celtics in 1957 and from 1959 to 1963.

The hallmark of a great passer is the number of assists he completes, passes which leave a team-mate with an easy, open, close range shot for basket. Cousy led the NBA in assists in every year between 1953 and 1960. Around 30 years after he finished playing. Cousy held records for the most assists in one half (19), the most free-throw attempts (32) and the most free throws made (30).

receiver, to deceive the defence or at least keep them guessing as to where the pass is heading
● Every pass in the open court should be made with the intention of progressing the ball down the floor towards the defenders' basket
● Any pass made while the receiver is closely guarded must be aimed to the side away from the defender, preferably to the receiver's outside shoulder area
● Never be lazy with a pass. A pass should always be made crisply and firmly
● Don't force passes. Every coach loves a creative passer but there is a thin line between forcing yourself to make an unwise or risky pass and creating an opening. Don't be afraid to make things happen but do it within the team concept
● Use ball fakes (page 81) before passing. Fake a pass to an area near your receiver before passing it to the exact point you want to reach

● Finally, and very importantly, make two-handed passes. One-handed passes are dangerous, because if an opponent steps in the way as you're moving your throwing arm you won't have the control to stop the pass.

Chest pass

Grip the ball with both hands by placing your fingertips on both sides of the ball with your thumbs almost meeting behind the ball. The elbows are slightly extended out from the side. Hold the ball around chest height and as you make the pass, step towards the receiver. When your arms are straight out in front of you, release the ball with a snap of the wrist. Your thumbs should end by pointing down at the floor. As the ball should travel in a straight line, the receiver should take the pass in the chest area.

This is the best pass to use while advancing the ball up the floor on a fast break when you zip the ball around the perimeter of your opponents' defence to make their players move around and leave gaps for shots.

As the ball goes in a straight line, remember you can use it only when no-one is in the way.

WHELTON'S TIPS

● *Good passing sets up high percentage shots*

● *Unselfish passing brings a team closer together and builds understanding*

● *Knowing how and when to pass makes good shooters into great shooters and average shooters much better*

Chest pass
1 Before making the pass, grip each side of the ball, with the thumbs almost meeting behind and the elbows extended ready to push off the ball and give protection while you prepare to make the pass

2 Step forward to make the pass with the arms extended on release and the thumbs pointing down at the floor

Bounce pass
1 The grip and release is the same as for the chest pass, except that you should aim to bounce the ball once off the floor about two-thirds of the distance between the passer and the receiver

2 and 3 The ball reaches the receiver at waist height, with backspin imparted by a flick of the wrist making the ball slower off the bounce and easier to catch

1

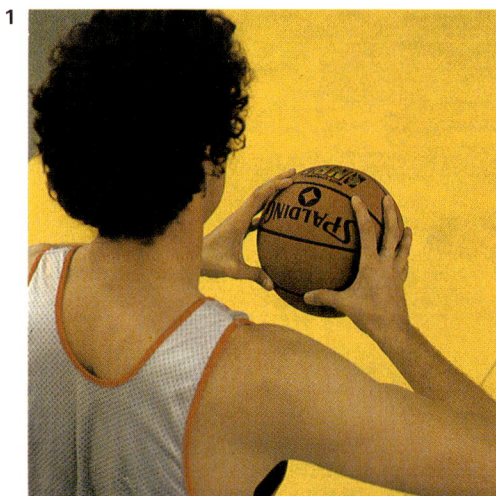

Bounce pass

The bounce pass is used to avoid a defender who is trying to block or intercept the ball. It is made in the same way as the chest pass but with the passer bouncing the ball once on the floor between him and his receiver. The bounce takes the ball past the defender, below his reach.

The grip for the two-handed bounce pass is identical to the chest pass. The release is the same but the ball bounces once, about two-thirds of the distance to the receiver and the ball should reach your team-mate at about waist height. The flick of the wrist on release of the ball creates backspin, which will make the ball a little slower off the bounce and help it to bounce high and be more easily caught.

2

3

Overhead or outlet pass

The overhead pass helps a player pass over a defender or a defensive trap and can also be used to reach a taller team-mate standing close to your opponents' basket. This pass may appear easy but it must be practised so that you can put some 'zip' on the ball because it must move fast through the air where, of course, it is more in danger of being intercepted or blocked.

The pass is made with two hands on the ball, as for the chest pass, but with your arms extended over your head. When you release the ball, snap the wrists to complete the pass with your fingers pointing towards the receiver and your palms facing the floor. The pass is easier to catch at head height or even a little higher. If your team-mate receives the ball lower than head height it becomes harder to handle.

Overhead or outlet pass
Put snap into the overhead pass, and release the ball with a 'snap' of the wrists ending with your fingers pointing at the receiver and your palms facing downwards

Baseball pass

This pass is made initially by having both hands on the ball, with one leg in front of the other and the opposite throwing arm directed towards the receiver. When ready to pass, bring the ball back on the throwing hand and then push off your back foot and release the ball with the arm extended and with a flick of the wrist. Follow through by bringing your arm forward after the ball is released.

After completing the pass the arm should be pointing at your receiver but your palm should be facing away from the rest of your body with the thumb pointing down to the floor. This action stops the ball from spinning sideways, which creates a curve on the path of the pass.

This pass is one of the most difficult to complete and needs lots of practice. It is also the one occasion when you can make a one-handed pass. But it should be done only when the player making the pass is standing out of bounds (out of court) and so not in danger of having the ball knocked away from him when he draws the throwing arm back over his head.

Overhead baseball pass drill
This is a long, down-court pass, usually made as part of a one-pass fast break offence. Teams that want to run a fast break must practise this pass as it's the quickest way to get the ball down the floor. The easiest way to practise is to have one player stand on the half-court line near the sideline and another player underneath the basket with the ball in his hands. This player puts the ball up into the basket. As the ball comes out of the net the other player simultaneously starts

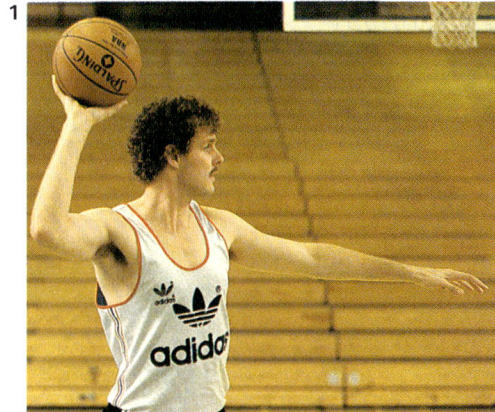

1

2

Baseball pass
1 and 2 The ball is initially held with two hands, but when you're ready to pass bring the ball back on to your throwing arm

his run towards the other basket. The player with the ball steps one pace out of bounds underneath the basket and then throws the baseball pass down court to meet the other player running in from the sideline to arrive at full stride under the other basket and ready to score.

> These passes are useful and exciting – but you're sure to be back on the bench if they go wrong

Danger passes

These passes can be very effective at creating openings but be careful when you use them or they could end with the ball going to the other team.

These passes should be attempted only when all the other passes have been mastered. They can be useful and are especially exciting to spectators. They are also a sure-fire way to be taken off the floor and put on the bench by the coach if they aren't completed or if the ball goes to the other team. All your coach and your team-mates want is that the play is completed no matter which way it is done, and the simpler passes are usually the most effective.

Jump pass

This is usually most effective when made by a good shooter. The element of surprise helps here because when he gets the ball the defenders will expect him to shoot. Instead the player jumps with the ball above his head as if to shoot at the basket, but passes from mid-air to a team-mate close to the basket or completely in the clear with an easy scoring chance. This pass is most successful when the offensive players fully understand the moves their team-mates will be making.

Touch pass

This is in the armoury of players who can read a situation in a fraction of a second. The danger is that the ball is never fully under control. As they receive a pass they instantly deflect the ball with their fingertips to an open team-mate.

Behind-the-back and between-the-legs passes

A behind-the-back pass is made when the ball hand is drawn back and the ball is passed across the small of the back to a team-mate standing to the other side of the passes. The between-the-legs pass is also made to either side of the passer. In the between-the-legs right-handed pass the ball passes behind the left leg, which is the lead leg. For the left-handed pass the ball passes behind the right leg.

PASSING CHECKLIST

- **Try to look away** *from your intended receivers, to deceive the defenders*

- **Aim** *your pass at the receiver's outside shoulder away from his defender*

- **Don't be lazy** *make your passes crisp and firm*

- **Passing tires out everyone** *on the defensive team, giving you better opportunities for clear shots*

Behind-the-back pass
1 Draw back the hand holding the ball

2 Pass the ball across the small of your back to a team-mate standing to the side of you

Passing
The ball-handler wants to make a right-handed pass so he moves his left leg forward

The ball makes one bounce just to the side of the lead leg

The ball rises after the bounce to be caught at chest height by a team-mate

Group passing practices

One-player drills
A player stands about 6 or 7 ft (2 m) from a solid wall and practises each pass by bouncing the ball off the wall. Next he chalks targets on the wall and makes the passes again while looking away from the target spots. This will improve peripheral vision and be an excellent practice for fooling opponents by looking at one point but passing the ball in another direction.

Two-player drills
The players start at one baseline, standing about 10 ft (3 m) apart. They run up and down the floor using crisp chest passes to move the ball between them. The object is to prevent the ball from touching the floor.

One player speed dribbles down to the opposite free-throw line where he makes a chest or bounce pass to the other player standing out on the wing who attempts a shot. The players reverse the roles and run back to the other basket.

Three-player drills
Players stand about 15 ft (4.5 m) apart with a defender in the middle. The offensive players must pass the ball to each other without the defender touching it. A player whose pass is intecepted becomes the defender who must try, in his turn, to intercept passes between the offensive players. This is a useful drill because it forces the passers to use the chest, bounce, overhead and touch passes to keep the ball moving.

Players start at one endline, spread far apart. The ball starts with the player in the centre of the line and the players run up the floor weaving in and out using the chest pass to move the ball between them. A player always immediately runs behind the man he passes to. This simulates a game because players are running and passing. The ball should not touch the floor.

Five-player drills
Five offensive players simulate a full-court fast break with no-one dribbling the ball. Start at one basket where the player throws the ball off the backboard, catches it and then throws an overhead outlet pass to a player who makes a chest pass to another player on the opposite side of the floor. He throws a bounce pass to the next player running in to attack the basket.

Ten-player drills
This is played only on half the court area with five offensive and five defensive players. The offensive team can't dribble and the race is to be the first team to score 50 points. A team scores one point for a completed pass and two for scoring a

field basket (page 124). The team that scores retains possession. The defensive team goes onto the offensive only after stealing the ball or taking a rebound (page 40).

Twelve-player drill
For this drill three players, with one ball between them, line up under each of the baskets. One player stands at each of the four 'elbows' where the foul line meets the lane which is drawn under the basket area. One player stands at each end of the halfway line, where it meets the sideline.

On the whistle, one player from each group of three under each basket takes the ball and makes a chest pass to the nearest player standing at the elbow. As the first player runs by him the elbow player passes the ball back, and the first player now makes a chest pass to the player standing on the halfway line. Again, the first player gets the ball back from another chest pass and, continuing up the court, he makes a chest pass to the elbow player standing at the other foul line.

When he gets the ball the first player runs into the other basket to score with a lay-up. All this time, of course, a player started from this end of the court and repeated the process with the players standing on the other foul lines and halfway line.

As soon as the player completes his pass sequence with a lay-up, one of the other players waiting under the basket collects the ball and starts off on his pass sequence. This drill can be varied to take into account the bounce pass.

All these drills can obviously help players to become better passers. But the most important thing is that you must *want* to be a passer. Most younger players don't understand how important passing is in building winning teams. Passing gets everyone on the floor involved with the play which makes the game more enjoyable to play and to watch.

PASSING PRACTICE CHECKLIST

● *One-handed passes are dangerous – use both hands*

● *Don't 'telegraph' your passes – mislead the defender with a 'fake' pass*

● *Pass to your team-mate's side away from his defender*

● *When the way is clear always move the ball down the floor, attacking the other basket*

● *Passing gets everyone involved. The more you give the ball up, the more you get it back*

Mechanics of shooting

There are different types of shot, but they all have the same pattern. Any player can attempt a shot but if he or she doesn't develop the confidence to shoot the ball there is no way that ball is going in the net. The only way to gain confidence is through practice. You must do the positive things over and over again, which means once you have the right technique, don't change and always shoot the same way.

These are the fundamental stages in completing any shot.

Anticipation

Before being able to take any shot you must anticipate where and when you will have the chance to shoot. The chance may come off a dribble or from a team-mate's pass – whatever happens, you must be ready. If the shot is at the end of your dribble you must end your dribble with your hands ready to shoot the ball. If your shot will be from a pass, receive the ball with your hands spread, ready to shoot immediately.

1 Pull up at the end of a dribble and look towards the basket to size up a shot

2 Gain your balance and start to lift the ball over your head, still concentrating on the basket

3 Without having taken your eyes of the basket, straighten your legs, with the ball over your head

4 You're off the ground with your legs straight, having released the shot at the top of your jump

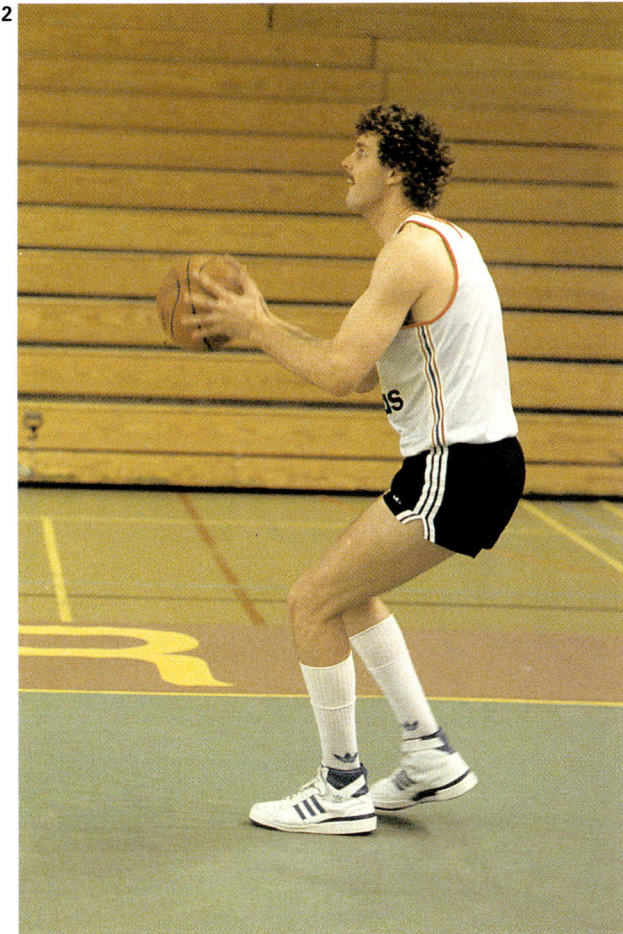

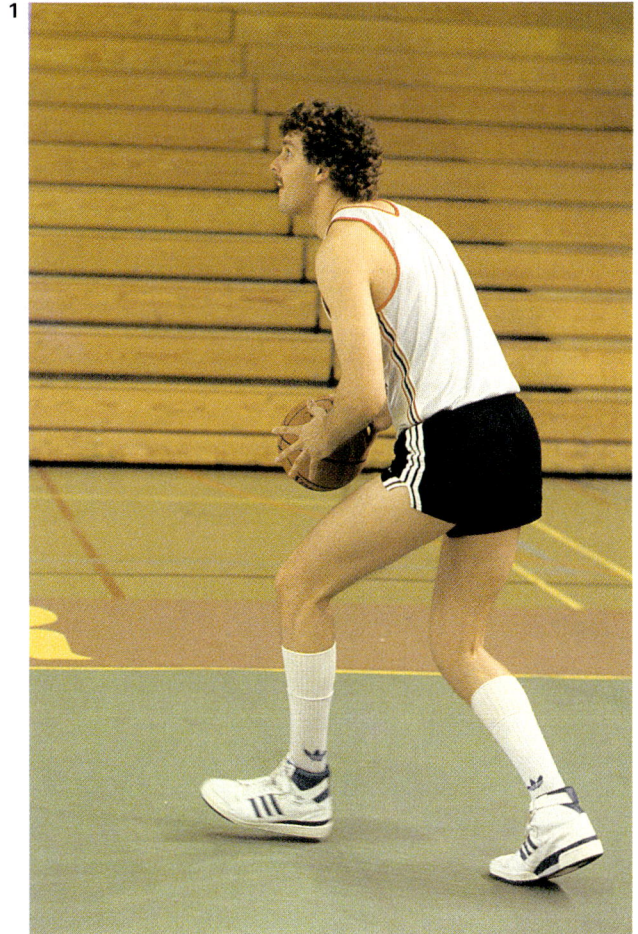

appears to be an uncomplicated challenge at first sight, offering the immediate reward of watching the ball swish through the net.

Opposite: A jump shot from 7 ft (2.1 m) Akeem 'The Dream' Olajuwon of the Houston Rockets. Kareem Abdul Jabbar of the Los Angeles Lakers, 7 ft 2 in (2.2 m), tries to block

Balance

When you have the opportunity to shoot you must position your body for the best possible chance of taking the 'perfect' shot. Be poised on the balls of your feet with your legs slightly bent at the knees, so that you can gently 'spring' or bounce up and down. You will have developed shooting technique in practice but now you must use your body strength mostly through your feet and legs to give you the balance to take the shot. An off-balance shot is usually a bad one, which means a low percentage shot with little chance of scoring.

Finding your spot

Before you release your shot you must decide where to shoot at. Most people call it aiming the ball, but I think it's more definite than that. It's literally picking out a spot, whether it's just over the front of the rim, the back of the rim, or on a part of the backboard – you must zero in on that spot.

I think that if you're shooting from in front of the basket or from the corners you should aim for just over the mid-front or part of the rim facing you. When shooting from the side of the basket or the wing areas of the court I suggest using the backboard to deflect the ball into the net. When shooting a lay-up (page 32), I believe you should always use the backboard as your aiming spot.

Release

Releasing the basketball is the crucial element in the mechanics of shooting. The moment of release most often determines whether the ball hits or misses the target. The ball should be released at the peak of your jump with both hands on the ball, one as the shooting hand and the other as the guide to steady the ball.

The fingers must be spread with their tips on the ball. You should be able to see a gap between your fingers and your hand. Your shooting arm should extend smoothly towards the basket as your arm becomes fully extended. Flick your wrists or 'wave goodbye' to the basketball as your hand snaps down to form a right angle with your forearm. The ball should roll off your fingertips as this action will give the ball a backwards rotation which is important in producing a 'soft touch' when the ball hits the ring of the basket and seems to dance on the rim. This gives the ball a chance to fall into the basket or at least leaves the ball close to the rim to give the offensive rebounders an opportunity to tip it into the net.

Follow-through

Follow-through is an important aspect of shooting. It's the grand finale to the perfect shot. You leave your arm extended, wrist snapped down, fingers pointing towards your aiming spot and your eyes still fixed on your target.

The flick of the wrist on release imparts backspin on the ball and gives the shot a 'soft' touch

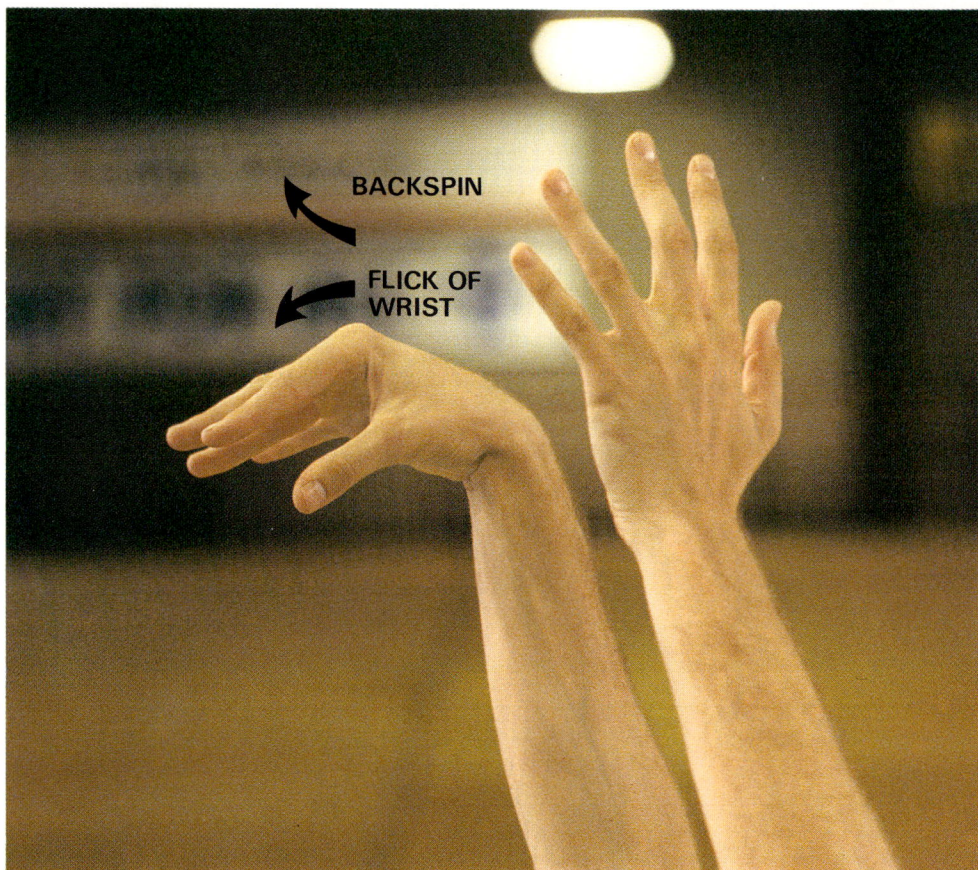

CHECK WORDS

Outside *Away from the basket and outside the lane area, which is the area drawn on the floor under the basket*
Inside *Close to or under the basket*

' The jump shot gives every player the opportunity to score from anywhere on the court '

Jump shot

The jump shot, or 'J', is the most common shot in basketball. It gives a player the opportunity to launch a shot from anywhere on the court. As you progress to higher levels of competition it's difficult to compete if you haven't got a jump shot. A tall player, who is expected to score from very close range, may develop a 'J' from only 10 to 15 ft (3 to 4.5 m) away from the basket but this will keep the defence working hard.

Jump shooting is a skill of basketball that will always be needed at all levels.

When striving for the perfect 'J' you must work hard on the mechanics of shooting and now we will expand on the points made earlier for general shooting technique.

Anticipation

With or without the ball you must anticipate where and when you will take your jump shot. If dribbling you must have your head up to see the floor ahead of you and how the game is developing. If you're leading a fast break down the middle of the floor, as when approaching the foul line (page 124), if no defender confronts you, you must be ready to shoot your jumper, or jump shot. Without the ball you may be on the 'weak' side of the floor (the opposite side from where the ball is, which is called the 'strong' side), using a team-mate who is creating space for you by blocking your defender. You must be ready for your team-mate with the ball to pass to you, and be ready to shoot at once.

Balance

Receive the ball with your knees bent to give you spring and your hands each side of the ball ready to shoot. After deciding to shoot you must use your legs and feet to give you the strength to balance yourself before releasing the ball. Keep your feet a shoulder's width apart, knees bent ready to spring, and 'square up' to the basket. Your head must look straight at the target with

STAR TIP

☆Even the legendary playmaker Magic Johnson of the Los Angeles Lakers had a weakness in an inconsistent outside jump shot. Opponents started to lay off Magic to try to take away his strength which was driving at the basket. Instead they wanted him to shoot from outside the key area where they were sure he was likely to miss. Through constant practice, over the years Magic has developed a sound outside 'J' which has helped to make him a more complete offensive player.

your shoulders square on and parallel to the basket. This squaring up is all important as it gives you balance before releasing the ball.

Finding your spot

After you start your vertical jump, launched from both feet, you must concentrate solely on the spot you've picked out. It may be just over the middle front part of the rim or it might be a spot on the backboard. If you feel comfortable use it. Before you release the ball you must have chosen either to swish the ball straight through the net or to use the backboard and you must stick with that decision. You mustn't change your mind half-way through the shot.

Release

Players might sometimes launch off balance and still score, but the release of the shot must be correct for the ball to go in. If you're right-handed the right hand becomes your shooting hand and the left hand is your guide hand. When taking a jump shot you want to release the ball at the peak of your jump. Your shooting arm extends towards the basket, your wrists snap down and the ball rolls off your fingertips giving it a backward rotation. The angle of the upward flight of the shot should be around 45 degrees.

Follow-through

Don't 'pull the string' on your jump-shot or, in other words, don't pull your shooting hand back immediately after releasing the ball. This action creates a hard shot. Instead you should wave goodbye to the ball with your arm extended and wrist flicked down, fingers pointing towards the target, producing a soft shot. Keep your eyes on the spot you're aiming for until the ball hits.

Practices
One-player drills

Spin the ball with both hands, creating a backwards rotation and allowing the ball to bounce once on the floor in front of you. Move towards the ball, pick it up off the bounce, balance by squaring up to the basket, find your spot, release and follow through. Retrieve the ball and repeat the process shooting from different places on the floor.

Two-player drills

One player is the rebounder and passes while the other player is the shooter. The shooter moves around the floor staying in shooting range, taking jump shots without dribbling the ball. The shooter must move after every shot. The rebounder must retrieve the shot and make a good overhead pass to the shooter. The shooter takes 20 shots, then exchanges roles with the rebounder. Also practise receiving the pass and using a one-handed dribble, either right or left, to improve this drill.

1 Make sure you're in the right position for the three-point shot, outside the arc

2 Lift the ball above your head, concentrating your aim on the target

3 Release the shot off a jump shot still keeping your eyes on the basket

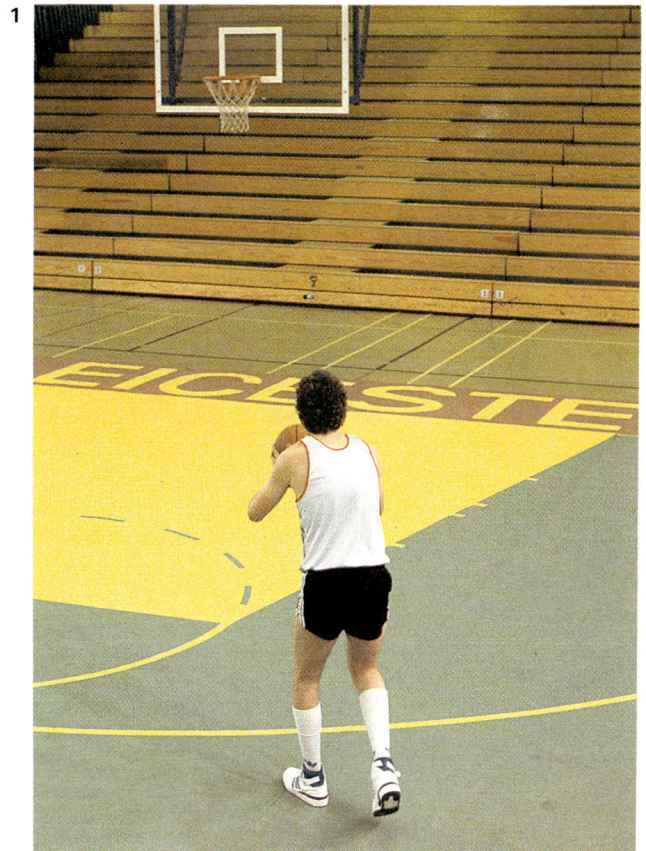

'One year my team was one point down in a championship final when we stole the ball in mid-court and a quick pass set one of my forwards dribbling to the basket with a defensive player in hot pursuit. Going at full speed, my player lost control of his lay-up and the ball hit the backboard far too hard and rebounded back into play. The defender got the ball and the other team scored again. No single missed basket costs a championship – but try telling that to my player. Players worried that their shot will get blocked alter their lay-up routine. You mustn't. Practise your lay-ups with both hands, going full speed at the basket '

Lay-up shot

The lay-up is the easiest shot in basketball to master and the shot that players take when finishing a fast break. Lay-ups are also used by teams to get their muscles warm and loose in pre-game routines. The only time the lay-up becomes difficult is when you must shoot under pressure

from a defender chasing you. Players worried that their shot may get blocked tend to hurry or alter their lay-up routine. That is why you must spend a great deal of time practising your lay-ups at full speed by going hard towards the basket to master the shot with both hands.

Anticipation

When dribbling towards the basket you must be moving fast but under control. As you approach the basket move slightly to one side of the hoop, giving youself a good angle to use the backboard for your shot. Going straight at the basket makes it more difficult to use the backboard as the ball may bounce off the back of the rim or skim off the front of the rim.

If you're running down the floor without the ball, stay wide of the ball-handler to give yourself the angle you need to run in after receiving his pass. At the extended foul line area anticipate the pass by having your hands ready to catch the pass without breaking stride.

Balance

This is where the lay-up is either made or missed. You shouldn't be out of control when releasing the ball because although the lay-up should be an easy shot, the ball still has to be laid up softly even though you're running at full speed.

As you stride towards the backboard, you should initially take a three-quarter step with your outside foot (the one furthest from the basket) and then a full stride with your inside foot pushing off the floor. When leaving the floor keep

your outside knee bent to help you maintain balance. Go towards the basket with your head and eyes up. Always protect the ball by keeping two hands on it and keep the ball slightly to the outside away from the basket. Remember the defender is most likely to be running down the middle of the floor trying to steal or block the ball as you lay it up.

Finding your spot
Pick your own spot on the backboard about 8 to 10 in (20–25 cm) over the rim and slightly your side of the centre of the board. As with any other shot, you shouldn't take your eyes off your spot until the ball has made contact.

Release
There are two ways to release the basketball for a lay-up. The push shot is good for young players who need the strength to get the ball up to the basket. The push shot is released with the back of your hands facing you and your arm extended as you push the ball up to the basket off your fingertips. The underhand shot is best because it gives you the chance to lay the ball up softly. The ball is released with your palm facing up and your arm extended. The ball rolls off your palm, then your fingertips and you lay the ball softly against the backboard for it to drop down into the basket. The mechanics are still the same for both shots. Keep both hands on the ball until you're at the peak of your jump, then extend your shooting arm while releasing your guide hand. When your arm is fully extended the ball is released.

Follow-through
The follow-through for the lay-up is the continuous motion of your run and shot which will bring you underneath the basket.

Practices
One-player drills
Start from half court and dribble the ball as fast as you can, but under control, towards the basket. Dribble with your right hand and come in from the right side and lay the ball up and into the basket. Remember when shooting a lay-up right-handed you push up with your left foot. Retrieve the ball and dribble to half court. Turn and dribble with your left hand and take a left-handed lay-up by pushing off with your right foot.

Two-player drills
Repeat the same drill but with a second player standing in the lane as a defender. He should alter his defensive strategy for every attempted lay-up, that is try to block, try to steal, yell and even bump the offensive player to force him to concentrate on completing the lay-up.

Three-player drills
Once again, start at half court with one player in the middle of the floor with the ball, one player wide to his right and the other wide to his left. The dribbler goes towards the basket but stops at the foul line and makes either a bounce or a chest pass to one of his team-mates who catches the ball and strides in for a lay-up, ideally without taking a dribble.

Lay-up shot
1 Move in on the basket and make sure you're already concentrating on the target

2 Stride forward with the left leg to provide for the lift off towards the basket

3 Push off with the left leg, raise the right knee for balance and lift the ball towards the basket with your right arm

4 Lay the ball gently against the backboard, under total control even though it is at the end of a run

5 Roll the ball off your fingertips against the backboard or softly into the basket

STAR TIP

☆Shoot, shoot and shoot some more. Always try to practise foul shots when you're tired as this will simulate game conditions.

Foul shot (or free throw)

The foul shot is a free shot awarded to you because one of your opponents has committed a foul. It may be the most under-rated shot in basketball. Players and fans sometimes don't realize the importance of making foul shots. But ask any coach what drives them crazy and I'm sure that most will say 'he missed the foul shots'. Most teams average 65 to 70 per cent of their shots from the foul line and many games are decided in the last few minutes by which team can score foul shots while under pressure. So many players find themselves being either the hero or the villain at the foul line.

The only way to become a good foul shooter is to practise. Why put yourself into the embarrassing situation late in the game of missing the shot and losing the match. Get out there and practise! During the off-season while practising take 100 foul shots and during the season take at least 50 shots after the practice session as it is always better to practise foul shots while you're tired, since you're bound to be tired during the game. Foul shooting involves repetition and rhythm; doing the same things every time and reaching a comfortable fluid motion with your shot. Practice, repetition and rhythm will bring you the final part in binding together your free-throw shooting and that is confidence, which will carry you through the pressure moments of the game so you know you're going to make the shot when it counts.

Anticipation

The foul shot has been called, the official looks at the scorers' table to indicate who committed the foul and how many shots you will be awarded unhindered from the free-throw line. This is when you get yourself ready. It starts with a mental process of blocking everything else out of your mind except the foul shot. Don't think about the score, the time, the opposing fans who may be taunting you – just get yourself ready. I've seen players reach for a towel to dry their hands, wipe their hands on their socks or the soles of their sneakers or lick their fingertips. You will find different players perform the same ritual every

All players must compose themselves on the free-throw line before taking a shot at the basket. Usually they will have earned the foul by some fast, hard and often quite violent action. If you rush to the line to make an immediate attempt on the basket you'll probably miss. So, build a rhythm which you're comfortable following, and stick to it. Whatever it is, taking deep breaths, lifting then dropping the shoulders or bouncing the ball a set number of times, make it *your* routine and run through it every time you practise and every time you go to the line during a match

time. This is the start of repetition and building a rhythm to your free-shot routine.

There's no hurry to get to the foul line so take your time and catch your breath. When the official hands you the ball you have up to ten seconds to shoot, depending on the rules you're playing under. Under international rules you have five seconds. But don't worry – that's plenty of time.

Balance

You're at the line with the ball. Now get ready to shoot. Step up to the line and set your feet shoulder-width apart, take a deep breath and exhale to relax your body. Then get into your rhythm. Some players just receive the ball from the official and shoot it immediately, while other players have a ritual of bouncing the ball, always the same number of times. Whatever it takes to make you feel relaxed and confident, do it. Don't change your routine: maintain the habit of doing the same thing every time.

Finding your spot

Some players aim for the back of the rim but I tell my players to look at the front rim and try to shoot the ball just over the edge of it. In lining up, try to have your right foot (if right-handed) pointed towards the middle of the basket as this will help you to line up your shooting arm when the ball is released.

Release

Have both your hands on the ball ready to shoot, bend your knees slightly with your eyes on the rim, bring your body up while straightening your knees and arms simultaneously and at the peak snap your wrists, rolling the ball off your fingertips. I advise against jumping when shooting a foul shot. Take a set shot, with your feet on the ground. Younger players, though, may need to jump until they get stronger.

Follow-through

Don't take your eyes off your spot until the ball has touched. You should exaggerate your follow-through by leaving your arm outstretched and wrist snapped down until the ball has hit the target. This follow-through action will hold your shot together, especially when you're tired during the game.

Hook shot

The hook shot is the forgotten shot of basketball. In the 1950s and 1960s it seemed as if every tall player had a hook shot and why not, since it is the most difficult shot to block. Although the hook shot is the most difficult shot to master, the extra practice will certainly give you a valuable weapon close to the basket.

Anticipation

A hook shot is taken when the offensive player has his back to the basket. Often when trying to free yourself from a defender you find you can get open and receive the ball with your back to the defender and the basket. When close to the hoop you must react quickly and the hook may help to release that quick shot. Anticipate receiving the ball and what you're going to do with it.

Balance

Receive the ball with both feet planted firmly on the floor with your knees slightly bent and have both hands on the ball at about chest height, with the elbows out to protect the ball. This position gets you balanced so you can hook either right or left-handed. When taking a right-hand hook shot take a small step to the side with your left foot while turning your body so your left shoulder faces the basket. Bring the ball up, releasing your left hand which then protects the ball from the defender who is between you and the basket. The ball is resting on the fingers of your right hand.

Finding your spot

'Look before you hook' is the common phrase of players with a hook shot in their array of offensive moves. Like any shot you must aim by finding a spot on the rim or backboard before you release the ball. In the balance stage of your hook, you turn your body to get in position to shoot and as you turn, your eyes should focus on the spot you want the ball to touch.

Release

Push off with your left leg, bringing your right knee up to give you more momentum. Your shooting arm should move towards the basket in an arc, and at the peak of your jump with the ball at the top of the arc you shoot by snapping your wrist and letting the ball roll off your fingertips.

Follow-through

Your body should follow through with your shot. The shooting hand should end up palm down, your feet should be planted on the floor with your head and shoulders square to the basket.

Practices
One-player drill

Move to different spots on the floor, close to the basket with your back to the hoop. Spin the ball out with backspin so it bounces back to around your waist height. Grab the ball with both hands, and take a hook shot. You must practise hooks with both right and left hands.

Two-player drill

Use the same drill but with a second player passing the ball to the shooter.

Three-player drill

Use a third player as a defender to try and pressure you as you're shooting.

Jump hook shot

This is an offspring of the traditional hook shot. The jump hook has become a very effective shot as players have become taller, stronger and more athletic. Offensive players have had to be more creative to launch their shot. Nobody wants to have their shot blocked and the jump hook is a quicker shot than the traditional hook and just as effective when done properly.

Technique

The only difference between a jump hook and a traditional hook is at the balance and release stage. For a right-handed shot instead of stepping out with your left foot, you turn your left shoulder to the hoop and push off with both feet straight up into the air with your guiding left hand releasing the ball as you jump.

In the release have your arm straight up in the air, releasing once again with a snap of the wrist. The tips of your fingers should be pointed towards the basket. The jump hook gives you the same advantages as the traditional hook in that your body is a shield to protect the ball from the defender.

Practices

Use the same drills as for the hook shot substituting the double-footed jump for the jump hook. And maybe one day you'll be as famous as Kareem Abdul Jabbar.

Dunk shot

The dunk shot is the most crowd-pleasing play in basketball, even more so than the three-pointer (page 125), the block (page 44) or the fancy assist (page 124). If lifts people out of their seats and can definitely help swing the momentum of a game from one team to another. Until the mid-1970s dunking was banned in American college basketball. I think the ban forced taller players to develop a variety and finesse to their game, utilizing hook shots and short jump shots. But today most coaches at the higher levels are teaching their players to dunk. It can be a high percentage shot and also a good way to get to the free-throw line by drawing fouls from defenders. It also intimidates opponents.

The dunk, like any other shot, needs to be practised. When you see some spine-tingling dunks by Michael Jordan of the Chicago Bulls, Dominique Wilkins of the Atlanta Hawks or even his team-mate Spud Webb, you must understand that they know from their continual practice exactly what they're going to do.

One of the most embarrassing moments is when a player misses a dunk. He usually stops and blushes or immediately fakes an injury. Don't dunk unless you've mastered the skill. Remember the dunk is the most difficult shot in the game. So before you risk any of those embarrassing moments out on the court in front of a crowd, make sure you know what you're doing.

Jump hook shot
1 Your arm should be straight in the air when you release the jump hook shot

2 Release the ball with your fingers pointing towards the basket

Burton drill

Use the screen

Burton drill
This involves dribbling, shooting and then passing to a team-mate

Use the screen
A dribbler who is being chased by a defender uses the 'screen', a team-mate without the ball, to shake off the chasing defender

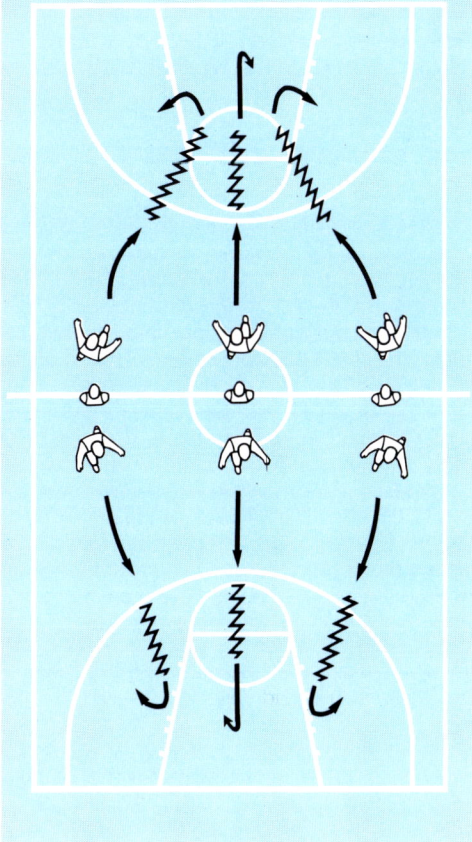

One player in each line dribbles towards one basket and shoots. At the same time one player in each line dribbles to the other basket and shoots. The players retrieve their own shot and dribble returning to half court, passing to the open player in their group and then receiving a pass from the other player to continue dribbling to the other end to shoot. After two or three minutes, the groups change spots on the floor.

Use the screen

A 'pick' or 'screen' is an offensive player without the ball who takes up a stationary position to defend a team-mate dribbling with the ball. The dribbler brushes past his pick, so that the defensive player chasing him crashes into the pick. Players split into groups of threes, with six to a basket, one passer, one screener and one shooter. The shooter is at the low post (close to the basket). The screener is at the high post (at the top of the key area) and the passer is also at the top of the key but to one side.

The screener goes down to set a 'pick' (page 84). The shooter uses the pick by brushing shoulders with his team-mate screener and then flashes out to the wing area. He receives the pass from the passer, squares up to the basket and shoots, following in his shot. Players may alternate spots after taking five to ten shots.

SHOOTING CHECKLIST

● **Anticipate** *Be ready to shoot immediately you receive the ball; always be a threat*

● **Balance** *Be on the balls of your feet, spread shoulder-width apart, knees slightly bent*

● **Find your spot** *on the backboard or the rim and zero in*

● **Release** *Shoot at the peak of your jump, extend your shooting arm towards the basket, then take your guide hand away*

● **Wave goodbye** *Snap your wrist down and wave goodbye to the ball as it rolls off your fingertips, imparting the back-spin which will create a 'soft' shot*

● **Follow through** *Leave your arm extended, wrist snapped down and your eyes fixed on the aiming spot*

CHECK WORDS

Fast break *A quick attack executed before the opposition take up their defensive positions*
Weak side *The opposite side of the offence to where the ball is being held*
Strong side *The side of the offence where the ball is held*
Screen or pick *Offensive player without the ball who blocks the path of a defender who is chasing the dribbler (usually) or another offensive player without the ball*

REBOUNDING

Rebounding is catching the ball after a shot has missed the basket and bounces back into play off the backboard or rim. It is one aspect of basketball that demolishes the myth that the game is a non-contact sport.

A team can't score unless it has the ball and pounding the boards is what gives you the ball. If your team dominates the boards you've gone a long way towards winning the match. Rebounding, of course, takes into account such physical attributes as height, strength and quickness. But the one element that is common in every great rebounder has nothing to do with physical prowess. It is the desire to play every shot as a missed shot; the desire never to quit; the desire to pull a rebound away from everyone else.

Some of the professional NBA's greatest rebounders have been 6 ft 6–8 in (1.98–2.03 m) tall and by no means the tallest men on the court. These players make the most of their potential by giving all they can to rebounding. The 1986–87 NBA season had 6 ft 6 in (1.98 m) forward Charles Barkley of the Philadelphia 76ers and 6 ft 8 in (2.03 m) Buck Williams of the New Jersey Nets as the league's leading rebounders. These players didn't rebound by waiting for the ball to come to them – they aggressively went out and got it. Many people consider Larry Bird the best player in the world, not only for his outstanding shooting and passing abilities but because he is also a very under-rated rebounder – and Larry can hardly jump!

Although it may seem as though some players are natural rebounders, that is not so. Just like any other skill in basketball, rebounding must be practised. It's essential to work on fundamentals and fitness. You have to learn to box out or block out (page 124), and you have to be in better shape than your opponents. You have to outwork your opponent during games so you must start during your practice sessions. Hard work in this area of the game has paid off for many players but for none more than Moses Malone. Moses, formerly of the Houston Rockets and the Philadelphia 76ers and then with the Washington Bullets, was probably the most dominant rebounder in the NBA for ten years from the mid-1970s. It is no coincidence that both the Rockets and the 76ers made it to the NBA finals with Philly actually winning the title. To watch Malone's consummate rebounding technique is as fine an example to younger players as can be seen.

Take a rebound as high as possible, at the peak of your jump

MOSES MALONE

★*Moses Eugene Malone, 6 ft 10 in (2.08 m) tall, was the best rebounder in the NBA in 1979, and from 1981 to 1985. He was also named the NBA's Most Valuable Player in 1979, 1982 and 1983. Malone was born in Petersburg, Virginia, and began his professional career with Utah, then played for St Louis, Portland, Buffalo, Houston, Philadelphia and then Washington.*

it's yours and he will want to find out early on what you're made of. Contact means to block out!

Some players block by stepping in front of their opponents and using their forearm to make contact with the player's upper body. Other players pivot with one foot while turning their back into the oncoming offensive player. The main point is to make contact and to stop the offensive player's clear path to the basket. Once you have slowed his momentum the fight begins.

● **Containing** – You've bumped each other – now guard your area. Don't be pushed underneath the basket. Contain your opponent by facing the basket with your eyes on the ball and maintaining contact with your opponent on your back. Hold him off by taking a semi-crouch position, feet spread more than the width of your shoulders with your arms up and elbows out and your feet moving in short stutter steps. This stance should give you a wide base to maintain your position.

● **Explosion** – Your blocking out stance will help you push off the floor to grab the ball. Once you've located the ball and it's within range, explode off your toes to reach up and grab it.

● **Possession** – Your team needs possession and they're counting on you. So use both hands to hold the ball. Be strong and expect contact from your opponent once you've got the ball.

● **Protection** – You've worked hard to get the ball so don't lose it. After gathering the ball with both hands come down with your feet spread and elbows out. Don't let anyone take the ball off you. Be aggressive and they'll get the message.

Rebound and outlet pass

We've discussed the six fundamental points essential to defensive rebounding, so now let's talk about the outlet pass. A correct outlet pass is the culmination of the rebound and at its best can be devastating. It is the foundation of a successful fast break.

The crucial point about the outlet pass is not to lose possession for your team. Don't take the risk of throwing the ball away. The guards, the ball-handlers who run the ball up the floor, must be prepared to come back to get the ball from the rebounder, because the rebounder has done his job once he has the ball in his hands and he shouldn't be left to make a bad decision under pressure. The guards must get free from the players guarding them even if it means coming all the way back to the rebounder and literally taking the ball out of his hands. Remember, although you always want to get as far down court as quickly as possible you can't score if you don't take the ball with you.

After the rebounder has the ball he comes back to the court with both feet planted firmly on the floor, with his back to his own basket. If you're rebounding on the left side of the hoop, pivot on your left foot and take a big step with your right foot towards the sideline. Turn your body to look up court with the ball held over your head and your elbows out. If you spot an open team-mate snap your wrists to make an overhead pass. The ball should be zipped through the air, not lobbed, which takes longer over the same distance.

If rebounding on the right side, pivot with your right foot. If the defender is guarding you closely, you can do one of two things. First make a good hard ball fake and then crouch under his arm and make a two-handed bounce or chest pass. The second option is to make an escape dribble. This again avoids the defender by taking one big dribble towards the sideline and then trying to find help.

Whatever you do, don't panic. The guards will help you. I believe it's easier to find guards who can get open or find the space to receive, than to find tall players who can rebound.

3 The defender turns and looks for a team-mate . . .

4 . . . and makes the outlet pass

CHECK WORD

Boxing or blocking out *Taking up a position and stance to prevent an opponent getting close to the basket*

Offensive rebounding

How often have I heard coaches talk after a defeat about their team having allowed the opposition too many second chances. These chances come from offensive rebounding, an ability few players have but nevertheless one that all can work on and develop.

Your opponents work very hard on defence trying to stop you and when your team finally launches a shot despite their good defence, what happens? One of your team-mates, by using clever moves against his defender, jumps up to tip the ball into the basket after the first shot bounces back off the rim. By outmanoeuvring the opposition you will have demoralized them and gained a lot more than just two points; in theory the defensive rebounder should have the advantage since he initially has the better position. But if your team executes their plays well the offensive rebounders have an opportunity to get a hand on the ball.

Teams' offences should be set up to get the most out of players' talents. The plays are set up for the jump shooters to take jump shots, for the low post (see page 48) people to receive the ball down low, and for the rebounders to be close to the basket.

Remember the offensive players have the benefit of knowing each other's habits and so can anticipate where and when the shots will come from.

This sense of when to move into rebounding positions can give the offensive rebounders a distinct advantage.

The easiest way to take an offensive rebound is to follow your own shot towards the basket. There are two reasons for this. Firstly, after releasing the ball you can tell immediately if it's going to be short or long or whether the ball will hit the rim to the left or right. Secondly, for the defender the act of getting a hand up to distract you then turning and trying to block out to prevent you from getting close to the basket, can be difficult and can leave him off balance, which will leave the offensive rebounder with the chance to go past him.

There's also the chance that the defender will lose concentration and look the other way down the floor, because he assumes that the shot has gone in.

If your team-mate takes a shot don't just stand there, move your feet and try to get around the defender. Fake one way with a short jab step, then go around him the other way. Another method is to make contact with the defender's back and spin past him by using a reverse pivot. Whatever you do don't push him in the back for a foul.

If you can't get both hands on the ball just try and keep the ball alive. If you can get position to control the ball with one hand try to tip it back into the basket. If this isn't possible tip it back out to a team-mate.

Offensive rebounding
1 The offensive player, closest to the camera, allows the defender to 'feel' him making a move to the right

2 Then the offensive player makes his positive move to the left, gaining the room to attack the basket

3 The shot has rebounded from the backboard and the offensive player is there first . . .

4 . . . to put the ball back into the basket

4

PAUL SILAS

★ Paul Silas was one of the NBA's great artists when it came to offensive rebounding. Silas's wonderful sense for the ball and his overwhelming desire always to be the first one ready to grab the missed shot gave him a 16-year career in the NBA. There were plenty of players in the NBA with greater natural ability than Silas, who at 6 ft 7 in (2 m) was by no means among the tallest players in the League. But his determination to get to the ball gave him a longer and more successful career than many players with far greater individual talent and ability.

Silas was born in 1943 in Arizona and after high school went to Creigton University in Omaha, Nebraska. Even then he was building his reputation as one of basketball's great rebounders. He still holds the record for most rebounds in a three-year college career. He was American college basketball's leading rebounder in 1963 and is one of only seven college players to average 20 points and 20 rebounds in a season.

His NBA career was with St Louis, Atlanta, Phoenix, Boston, Denver and Seattle as a player and he coached for three seasons with San Diego.

3

Rebounding drills

Rebounding is a skill that will benefit from determination and improved technique. Firstly, you have to want to rebound and secondly you must know all the tricks in the book to give you an advantage over your opponent. Rebounding depends on aggression and here are some drills that combine fundamental skills with developing that aggression.

Tip drill
This is good for timing, jumping and ball control. Start at the right side of the basket with a ball in your hands. Loft the ball against the backboard and jump with your right arm outstretched. Tap the ball off the backboard ten times by controlling the ball with your fingertips and flicking your wrists as if making a shot. You land on the floor after every tap and explode back up on the eleventh tap trying to tip the ball into the basket – don't stop until the ball goes into the hoop. After tapping with the right hand move to the left and repeat the drill using your left hand.

One-on-one block-out
Have one offensive player without the ball facing the basket at the foul line and one defensive player a few feet away to the side. The coach with

the ball stands to either the right or the left wing and takes a shot. The offensive player must do anything possible to reach the ball as must the defensive player, who is trying to block out. Have both players go after the ball even if it goes through the hoop. This develops good habits because rebounders must always assume every shot will miss and will therefore be ready to go for the rebound every time.

Two-on-two block-out
This drill requires four players. Have offensive player 1 stand on the right wing at least 15 ft (4.5 m) from the basket with offensive player 2 the same distance away on the left wing. Both players are guarded by defensive players 1 and 2.

The coach stands at the top of the key with the ball and passes to offensive player 1 who is closely guarded. Defensive player 2 must get one foot in the lane, the key area under the basket. The coach may keep passing the ball then instruct one of the players to take a jump shot. Defensive players on the shooter must get a hand up then block out. His team-mate who is off his man must become weakside rebounder (away from the ball) by finding his man, blocking out and rebounding.

Split your team into pairs with a guard and a forward. Make it competitive by giving two points for an offensive rebound and one point for a defensive rebound.

Three-on-three drill
Team up into groups of three. Three players are on offence, three on defence and a coach has the ball. Instruct the offensive players to move and set picks (page 84). The coach takes a shot, sometimes immediately and sometimes after 10 to 20 seconds. Both teams fight for position with the team that gets the rebound staying on the floor waiting for the next team. The first team to take seven rebounds wins, with the losers having to do sprints up and down the court.

Two-on-two block-out
Two against two in the confined area under the basket is a good way of developing the aggression needed to supplement your fundamental rebounding skills

Two-on-two block out 1

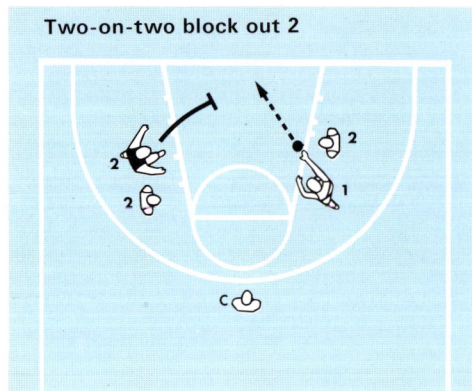
Two-on-two block out 2

KAREEM ABDUL JABBAR

★ *The fact that the Los Angeles Lakers were ready to give Kareem Abdul Jabbar a $2 million dollar contract to play at least two more seasons in the NBA at the age of 40, underlines the value of this player, arguably the greatest big man the game has ever seen. Born as plain Lew Alcindor, he went to Power Memorial High School in New York and then on to UCLA, the famed University of California at Los Angeles. Although Jabbar has made his name with Los Angeles club the Lakers, his first professional team was the Milwaukee Bucks. He was traded to the Lakers in 1975, winning six League Most Valuable Player awards and five championships.*

must realize which one of them is free and he is the one who must get the ball. Once the outlet pass is completed, all four players fast break down the floor hoping to score. It's a good idea to have two defensive players waiting down the other end.

Non-stop drill

This drill requires a coach to throw up the ball, three defensive rebounders and two offensive rebounders. The coach puts up a perimeter shot and the two offensive rebounders move into make contact with the back of two of the defensive rebounders. They have to work extra hard for position because there will always be an

extra defensive rebounder. After the offensive rebounders make contact with their defensive player, they must roll off him and use pivots to try and get position closer to the basket. This drill demands non-stop effort. If the offensive players get the rebound they either put the ball back into the basket or tip it away to the perimeter where their guards would be waiting during a game.

REBOUNDING CHECKLIST

● **Desire** *Assume every shot will miss and have the desire to get to the ball first*

● **Anticipate** *when and from where the shot will be coming, and be ready. But don't move until the ball is in the air*

● **Contact** *Block out the offensive player to stop him having a clear path to the basket*

● **Explode** *off your toes to reach up and grab the ball*

● **Keep it** *Use both hands to protect the ball and come down with feet spread and elbows out*

Non-stop drill

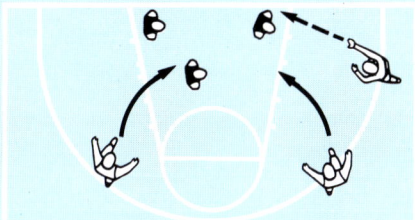
Non-stop drill

Outlet drill 3

Outlet drill 4

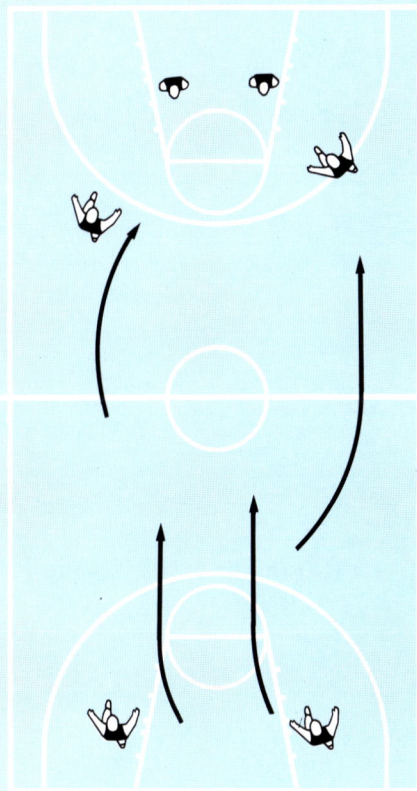

Non-stop drill
This requires hard work because there will always be an extra defender

Outlet drill 3
The outlet player has reached the halfway line and receives the pass

Outlet drill 4
He loads the fast break down the floor as the rest of the team catch up for a 4-on-2 offence

MAN-TO-MAN DEFENCE

Introduction

Man-to-man defence is the heart and soul of basketball. There is no better way to start winning than by playing effective man-to-man defence. There are occasions when even the greatest shooting teams will have an off night, but 'man' defence can be consistent through hard work and will carry a team through its bad patches when the ball doesn't go into the basket for them at the other end of the court. The teams that play successful man-to-man defence are the teams who are hard workers.

Players can't cut corners individually or as a team if they want to stop their opponents. Playing man defence is like having five fingers working together. Individually they have responsibilities but at all times they must work together. Some players are better guarding the player with the ball while others make better weakside defenders, but everyone must work to overcome their weaknesses. If one player skimps on the effort he is making the whole defence collapse – you can't have slackers! The players must be able to rely on each other and organize themselves. A team can't rely on one or two players to stop the opposing team, but must strive for team defence. Team defence is talking to each other on the floor, calling out the screens (page 125), helping out a team-mate who has been beaten, taking a charge from an offensive player. All these can help to develop an excellent man-to-man defensive team.

The type of man defence you use depends on the coach's philosophy and his or her understanding of their personnel. If a team has fast athletes I suggest trying to force opponents out of their offence by playing pressure defence. This is the idea of harassing the player with the ball and stopping the other four players from receiving the pass. This can be played full court or can be just as effective played at half court. If you have slower players a team might incorporate a 'sagging man' defence – guarding loosely and standing away from your opponents – where there is less risk of being beaten by quicker offensive players.

With the arrival of the three-point shot more and more teams have realized they must be able to play man defence. Although I like to use zones I believe that any rule that forces teams to play more man defence is good. The player who accepts his assignment in man defence and plays with intensity and determination is an ideal player.

The shooter's eye view of a 'hand in the face'

The defensive player, on the right, is watching both the offensive player on his right and anticipating the ball coming from his left

The offensive player makes contact

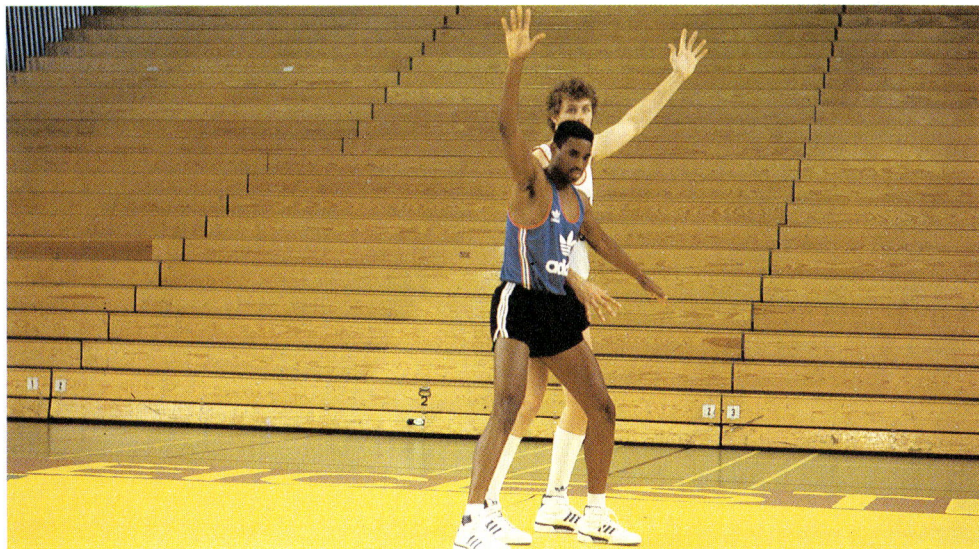

The defensive player pivots to front his opponent and to watch for the intended pass to the offensive player

The defensive stance –
feet spread, knees bent,
arms out in front, head
up and eyes on your
opponent's torso

Defensive stances

Correct stance on the ball and positioning off the ball are paramount to playing successful man-to-man defence. The basic defensive stance can alter slightly, but effectively the rules are the same.

● Feet spread, up on the balls of your feet – you can't play defence flat footed
● Knees bent at an acceptable level which doesn't leave you off balance
● Backside down to keep you low
● Back straight to help you balance
● Head up, eyes glued on your opponent's torso
● Arms out in front, elbows slightly bent with palms up so you can try to deflect the ball up in the air. This also stops you from slapping down which is almost automatically called a foul.

Although at first strenuous and a strain on your legs and back, eventually the defensive stance should feel comfortable. You should feel balanced which should help your speed off the mark, but you don't want to feel as if you're tipping to one side. Players can't practise the defensive stance too much. At times late in the season when practices are shorter I will still spend time working on the stance. It's a learned skill that needs to be continuously reinforced.

Footwork

At high school I had the chance to play for a great defensive coach, Stan Ogrodnick – now coach of Trinity College in Hartford, Connecticut. He taught us to use short choppy steps when guarding an opponent although most coaches use the 'step-slide' movement but both methods

work. The short steps are made with the balls of your feet in a constant up-down action not lifted more than half an inch, with the feet a shoulder's width apart. The step-slide motion is similar in that you want to maintain contact with the floor. The work is done from below the knee by a step-slide movement of the feet. Your knees and thighs shouldn't come closer than when you're stationary. In both cases you *never cross your feet*.

Don't ever run unless beaten in the open court. When this happens you turn and sprint; your goal being to get 4 to 5 feet (1–1.5 m) in front of the dribbler and then resume your defensive stance.

Guarding the dribbler

I think you should have your elbows to the side, bent so the forearms are out towards the offensive player with the palms up. Flick at the ball with an upward motion of the hands. If the ball is lowered in front of you go for it. Flick the ball up in the air and go after it aggressively.

Some teams prefer to have their arms and hands outstretched to the sides so that they can 'belly up' or get their midriff as close as possible to the dribbler. You need good speed to execute this otherwise you will foul.

When the dribbler stops and holds the ball overhead, one hand should follow the ball in a waving motion. If the ball is to one side, your nearest hand should be close to the ball with your other hand overhead, which will help you cover two areas.

If the dribbler jumps up to take a shot you should stretch your nearer arm as close to the ball as possible. If there's no chance to block the shot, quickly raise your hand near the shooter's face to distract his vision or concentration.

Guarding a player without the ball

The stance in this case is totally different. You are denying the passing lane, that is stopping the player from receiving a pass by blocking the path or lane the ball will travel along. This is the method of playing between the ball and your man, who you're defending. I tell our players always to try to stop a penetrating pass, which is a pass that will put the offence close to the basket. Although you can't always stop the pass, at least it may force the offensive player to receive the ball further away from the basket than he wanted to. To deny the passing lane you must play slightly away from your offensive man and get your outstretched arm and foot into the passing lane.

Don't get too close to the man you're guarding, or you will allow him to make contact with you and give him the advantage of being able to push away from you and leave you standing. You must see both where the ball is coming from and the man you're defending. This is done by focusing the eyes straight ahead and using your peripheral vision to see the movements of the ball and the player you're guarding.

The 'belly up' defensive stance, with the arms up straight and the torso pushed out at the offensive player

The defensive player's left hand has flicked upwards and knocked the ball out of the offensive player's hands

Front the offensive player by getting between him and the ball

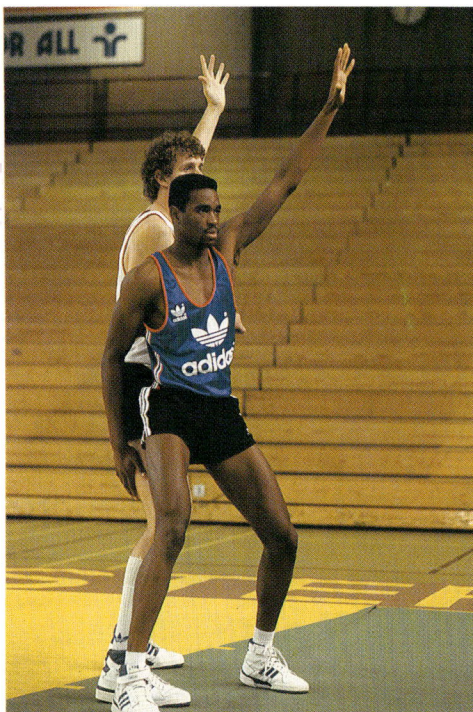

Play behind the offensive player and be ready to block his path to the basket if he gets the ball

Defending against post players

Playing defence against post players depends heavily on the coach's philosophy on playing man-to-man defence. I like our players to do the following when playing man defence in the post area.

Having the ball in the high-post area (near the free-throw line) makes defensive positioning difficult as there's no true weak side. When the ball handler is in the middle of the floor, he creates dangerous opportunities for the offence. In side fronting be positioned on the ball-side of your man: that is, with your body between the ball and your man. Crouch slightly, raised on the balls of your feet with one arm outstretched in the passing lane and your other arm outstretched pointing down behind the player. This is because you want to move closer to the offensive player and be brushing up alongside him. The rule of watching player and ball applies to all defensive stances.

If the offensive player is in the medium-post area, the area half way between the foul line and the basket, you as defenders should three-quarter front the player. This will help to keep the ball away from the post player and help you to retreat if the ball is lobbed over your head. This stance is similar to the side front, but you move your front leg further in front of the offensive player and have your front arm outstretched higher to deflect lob passes. Your front foot should still be level or behind the post player's nearer foot, since at the medium-post area there is room for a high or lob pass. This will at least give you a chance to retreat and regain a good defensive position.

When the offensive players assume the low-post area, close to the basket, strategies differ. Some teams with tall defensive players like to play behind the offensive player with their hands up, because the post player will have to shoot over a defensive player with outstretched arms and therefore put the defensive player in a ready-made rebounding position. Alternatively, full front the low post. The full-front defensive player, playing correctly, makes it nearly impossible to make a direct pass into the low post. Front by putting your whole body between your man and the ball, with your back to the man as you constantly 'feel' the player to gauge his movement.

If the post player has one leg forward towards you, put your opposite arm straight up into the passing lane, because, if he has one leg forward, it means he's trying to hold or seal you off for a lob pass.

The manoeuvring at the low post is a battle, with both players banging each other and trying to feel for position with hands, arms and back while keeping an eye out for passes.

Man-to-man defence drills

Shuffle drill
This drill can be used for one player or any number. One coach stands at the half-court line with the players spread out facing him. On a command the players must react quickly and get into the basic defensive stance. The coach may leave them in that stance for as little as 10 seconds or as long as 45.

The next step is to have the players use the step-slide movement on command. The coach will point either right or left with the players in the defensive stance quickly moving in each direction. The players should also practise going forwards and backwards, remembering never to run or cross their feet.

Zig-zag drill
This is a good drill to isolate each defender and pick out any errors in their defensive movements.

One offensive player with the ball starts on the endline facing up the floor, with the defensive player 2 to 3 ft (1 m) away in the defensive stance. On command the offensive player starts to dribble up the floor in a zig-zag pattern while the defensive player applies pressure without fouling, by forcing the dribbler to turn back or away. The players stop at the opposite endline and change roles. Start the dribbler off by going half speed then step up next time to three-quarter, then full speed.

Zig-zag, one-on-one drill
Start as for the zig-zag drill, but when the offensive player reaches half court he is allowed to go one-on-one against the defensive player. To make it realistic allow the offensive player no more than five dribbles after crossing the half court line. The defensive player must keep the dribbler to one side of the floor, stay in his stance, get a hand on the shot, block out but not foul.

Catch up drill
This drill is worthwhile because no matter how good a defensive player you are, during the course of the game you will be beaten and will need to recover. When a dribbler gets past you the tendency for most players is to get level with the offensive player and run alongside. This will almost always result in a foul being called. You want to sprint in front of the dribbler and give yourself enough room to turn and regain the defensive stance.

Start two players on the endline, one with the ball a step in front of the defensive player. The dribbler sprints down the floor. The defensive player, being a step behind, must sprint and get ahead of the dribbler, turn and play defence. The players play one-on-one to the basket.

Three-quarter front or stand to the side of the offensive player with your leading arm stretched across him to prevent the pass getting through, and your lead leg across the front of the offensive player

Side-front the offensive player, without having your lead leg across him or your arm stretching so far across

Denial defence
Preventing players from receiving a pass by blocking the path between them and the passer

1-4 As defensive player you must be ready to twist and turn in every direction, always 'feeling' for the position of the offensive player behind you, to maintain your readiness to intercept and block any pass into the basket area

Close out drill

It's a problem for the defence when an offensive player receives the ball 10 to 20 ft (3 to 6 m) away from the basket with no defensive player guarding him. The defensive player's first instinct is to sprint at the offensive player. This leads to an easy one-on-one move by the offensive player since the defensive player is out of control.

In this drill start a player without a ball at the top of the key facing the basket. The defensive player is standing underneath the basket with a ball. The defensive player rolls the ball rapidly out to the offensive player and sprints *halfway* to his opponent and then gets into his defensive stance using short choppy steps. The players go one-on-one, with the offensive player using no more than three dribbles. Sprinting only half way to your opponent allows you to take a controlled defensive stance.

Denial drill

This is a good drill for denying your opponent the ball by getting into the passing lane.

Have one offensive player without a ball in the wing area, one defensive player in the denial stance overplaying the passing lane and one coach with the ball to the right or left of the top of the key depending on where the players are. The coach tries to pass to the offensive player who is working hard to get free. The defensive player is overplaying, working on his stance and watching his opponent and the ball simultaneously. Don't worry about the player going back door (that is, along the base line under the basket) since in a game you will have weakside help from teammates away from the ball.

Post-denial drill

This incorporates two manoeuvres an offensive player may try against a defensive player on the same play. That is flashing to the ball in an attempt to receive a pass close to the basket and if not, posting up (taking position) strongly onto the low post and fighting for position.

A coach with the ball stands on one wing, the offensive players starts on the opposite low post and the defensive player is in the weakside position in the lane, pointing to the ball and his

opponent. The offensive player will flash out to try and receive the ball in the lane. If not he tries to post up on the low post nearest to the coach. The defensive player must see his opponent's move towards the ball and counteract it by bumping his opponent and denying him the ball. He then has to work at fronting his opponent once he moves to post up on the low post.

Numbers drill

Four offensive players line abreast across the foul line and foul line extended, face down court towards the other basket. Facing them are four defensive players, each with a number 1 to 4. The coach throws the ball to an offensive player and shouts a number, such as '1'. When this happens the four offensive players set off to the other basket, with three defensive players dropping back to guard them and defend the basket. But the player whose number was called out first has to run to the baseline behind the offensive players, then race back to catch up with the other players who are now attacking the other basket.

The fourth offensive player can try to steal the

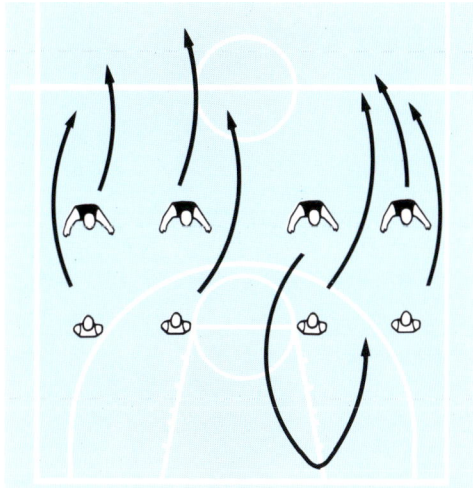

Numbers drill

Numbers drill
Four offensive players
and four defensive
players line up facing
each other

ball as he catches up with the offensive players. He also has to watch his three defensive team-mates to see where he can fit into their alignment.

CHECK WORDS

Pressure defence
Denying the pass and harassing the ball-handler
Press *Play pressure defence, over the full length of the court, half court or quarter court*

3

4

Team defence

Team defence is based on every player knowing and understanding why they have specific rules in man-to-man defence. Basketball is a game of adjustments, not only on the practice floor but more importantly on game night in the heat of the action. A coach has an allotted number of time-outs to get his tactics across to the players so they must understand what they are trying to accomplish. Therefore, before we set up our team defence let's discuss certain rules and terminology that will govern what happens.

Jump to the ball

**Over the top
1 and 2** The player defending the dribbler takes one big step around the screen

When guarding a player with the ball you mustn't think your job is over once he passes the ball to another player. Your concentration mustn't lapse

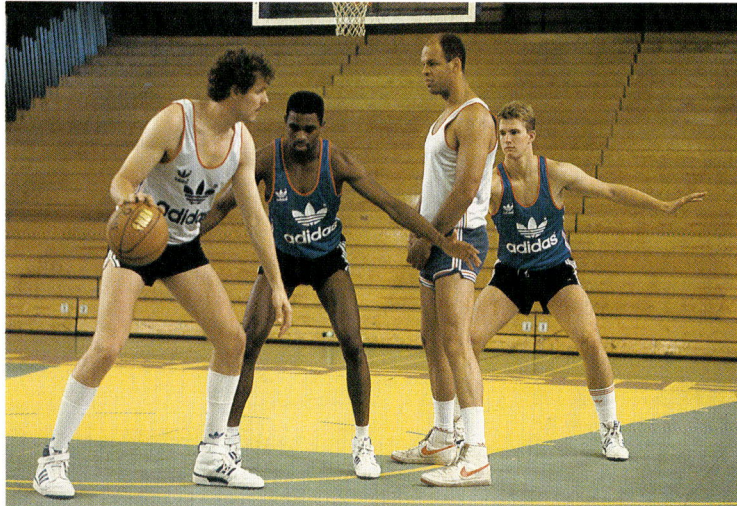

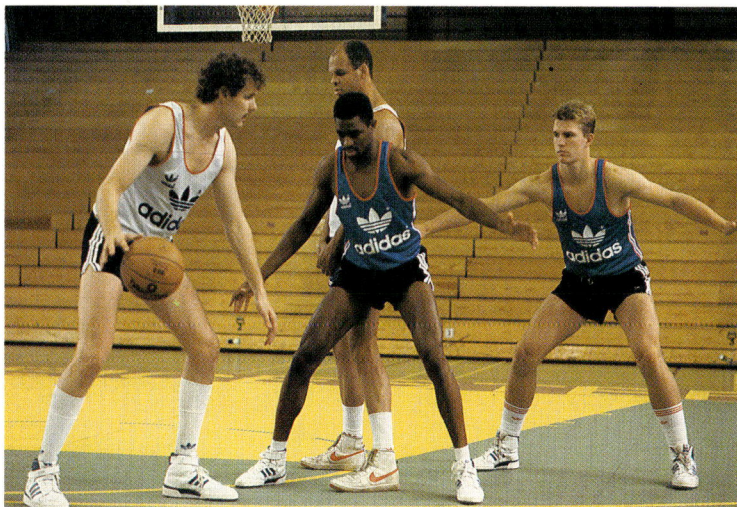

because he didn't score. A lapse could lead to a breakdown of the defence. When your opponent passes the ball you must jump to it, which means immediately taking a step back and towards the area the ball has been passed to, keeping an eye on the ball *and* your opponent. This movement will give you position to stop your opponent from cutting between you and the basket and put you in a position to help your team-mates.

Defending the pick and roll
Defending the pick and roll – when the pick rolls, or spins, round to face the basket and receive the pass from the dribbler – can be done in various ways but you must have specific rules.

Over the top
This is imperative especially when guarding a player who is in a scoring position and who has an outstanding jump shot. Firstly, the player guarding the screener must 'talk' – this is so important in team defence. He must warn the other defensive player where the screen is being set, shouting 'right' or 'left' to alert his team-mate where the screen is positioned. This call must be made early, loud and clear. When the defensive player hears the call he must put his hand out to feel for the pick, in other words feel where the opposing player who has set the pick is standing. To get over the pick he straightens up and takes one big step around the defensive player to prevent the screener moving between him and his opponent.

Once over the pick, he assumes his basic defensive stance on the ball. His team-mate defending the screener must 'help and recover,' meaning step out to guard the dribbler until he knows it's safe to return to guard his opponent.

Going through
This tactic may be used when the dribbler is too far from the basket to be in a scoring position or against a player who is not a scoring threat from the perimeter.

The defender of the screen tells his team-mate of the pick. The defender of the dribbler then feels for the pick, but this time he goes behind the screen and then picks his opponent up after the screen. The screen defender takes a step back which allows his team-mate to slide through.

Switch
This is a defensive coverage that some feel is an effective way to combat screens. Others fear that it is an easy way to let players play defence which will not always develop defensive toughness.

The defender of the dribbler feels the pick and yells 'switch', which is the key word for the screen defender to pick up the dribbler coming off the screen and stay with him.

One of the obvious weaknesses is that it creates mismatches which the opponent may take advantage of. Defending screens away from the ball can be done the same way. Players can go over the top of screens to keep intense pressure

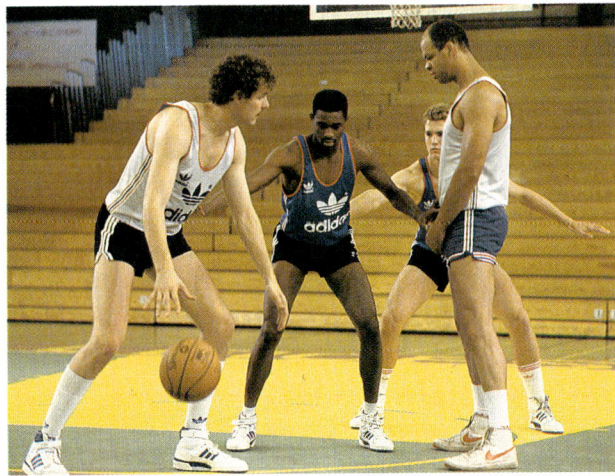

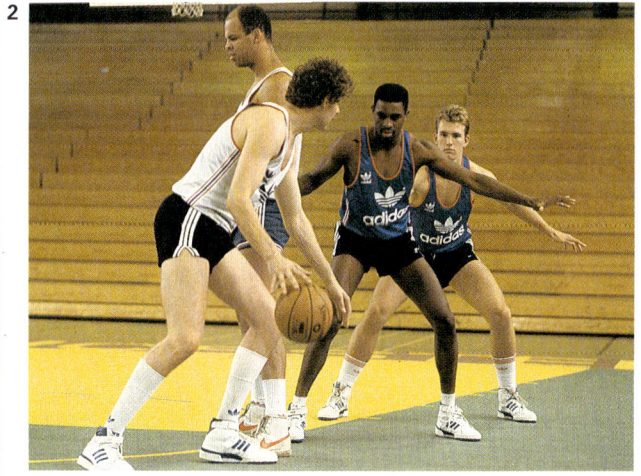

on the offence. They can go through to work for better positioning or they may switch to avoid getting caught on the screens.

Going through
1 and 2 The defender of the dribbler goes behind the screen to pick up his player on the other side

Switch
3 and 4 The defender of the dribbler feels the pick and yells 'switch', so the defender of the screen now picks up the dribbler

Man-to-man team defence

Man-to-man team defence can begin at different parts of the floor. You can use it full court, three-quarter court, half court or even a quarter court, depending on what you're trying to accomplish Whenever you pick up the offence you're going to have to stop them trying to score.

Let's put into operation all the rules we have talked about and develop a half-court man-to-man defence. Your defence starts on the ball. Meet the dribbler at half court and push him to the nearset sideline. In full or three-quarter court defence, zig-zag the dribbler to half court then push him to the sideline. Push the ball to one side to let your team-mate know who is strong side (the side of the floor the ball is on) and who on your defence is weakside as this helps you stick to your rules. The ball-handler is being harassed and not allowed to turn and dribble back across the floor and the wing defender is overplaying the passing lane, forcing the offensive player to go out of the key area or to receive the ball far away from the basket. The high post defender is side-fronting the high post, not letting the ball in. Your weakside defenders are about a third of the way between their opponents and the ball. They're 'pointing' one hand towards the ball and the other towards their opponent. This helps them see the ball and their opponent. Whenever a player is beaten by a dribbler the nearest defensive players must 'help', by which they all understand that the most dangerous player on the floor is the one with the ball. Defensive players must help stop the dribbler and then recover and find the player they're guarding.

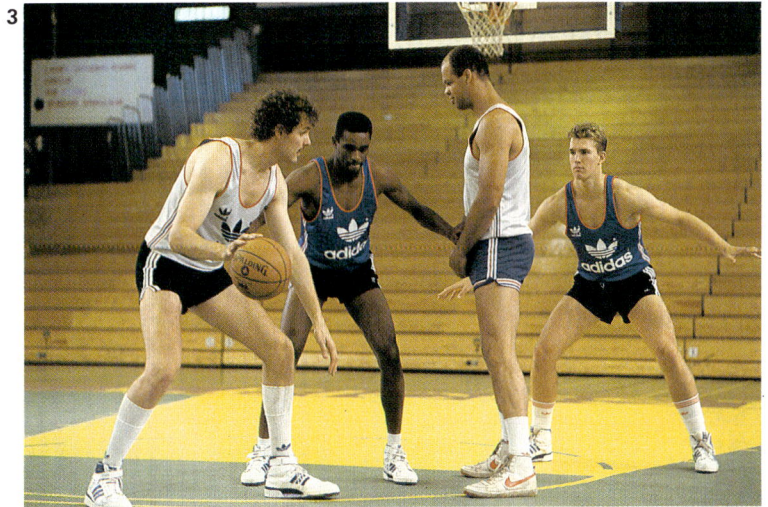

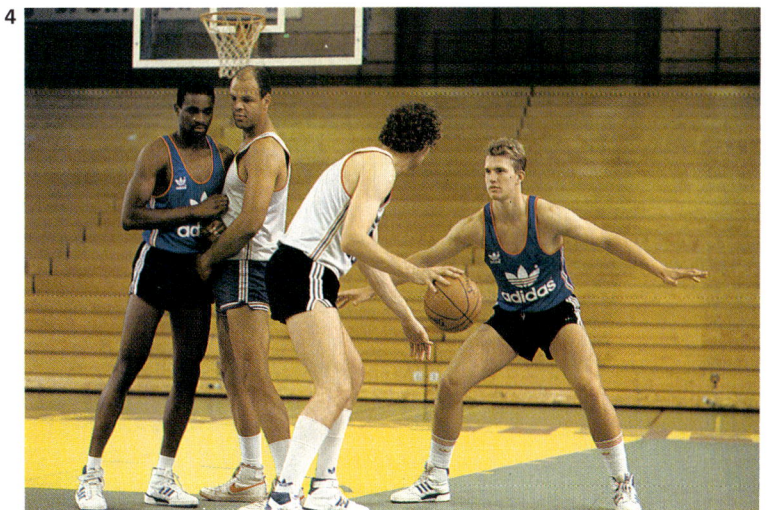

Team defence drills

Pick and roll defence drill

This is a good drill to practise against the pick and roll (page 84).

As shown in the diagram defensive player D1 is playing defence on offensive player O1 who has the ball. O2 and O3 are setting stationary screens at the foul line extended area, D2 and D3 are side fronting. As O1 dribbles towards one of the screens D2 and D3 start calling out the screens to D1. Depending on what you are working on, D1 must go over the top of the pick, go through, or switch with D2 or D3. O1 will use one pick then reverse and use the other, repeating and using each pick three or four times.

Three-on-three half court drill

Three-on-three half court drill
Defensive player 1, guarding the dribbler, must be ready to go over the top of the pick, go through the pick or switch with D2 or D3

Three-on-three continuous drill
Non-stop action is the main ingredient of this drill as players have to defend then make the transition into offence, while under pressure from a new set of defenders

Three-on-three half court drill

This drill involves three offensive players versus three defensive players. The offence starts with one player at the three-point line in the middle of the floor, with two other offensive players on opposite wings. The defensive player on the ball is pushing the dribbler to one sideline while the strong-side wing defender is overplaying the passing lane and the weakside lane defender is in the help position. The offence uses all tactics for three-man basketball such as give and go (page 84), pass and screen away (page 84), pick and roll (page 84). The defenders must communicate with each other while using defensive manoeuvres such as jumping to the ball, opening up on weakside screens, or defending the pick and roll.

Three-on-three continuous drill

This drill is good for defending, transition and conditioning. Players really enjoy this because of its competitiveness.

As shown in the diagram, 9 players are used although 12 or even 15 can take part. The teams are in groups of three. Try and group point guards, off guards and forward-centres. Offensive players O1, O2 and O3 have the ball first, attacking defensive players D1, D2 and D3. They play three-on-three basketball trying to score. Team D gets possession of the ball by a steal, rebound, charge, or successful basket by team O.

Once team D gets possession they immediately turn up court where the third team T are waiting at the half-court line ready to play defence. Once team T gets possession they go up court where team O are now waiting for them at half court.

The first team to score seven baskets are the winners. Defenders must pick up their player at the half-court line, as this prevents players trying to be lazy and cheat.

Shell drill

This is a drill that I believe must be used by every team that wants to play man-to-man defence. There are many variations of this drill so that you can work on just about any defensive tactic you want.

The shell drill is a great teaching tool because you can go one step at a time adding more steps as the team masters them. Here are some objectives you may try to master:

Three-on-three continuous drill

As shown in the first diagram there are two teams, O and D, with four players each. The ball starts on either side of the floor with either O1 or O2.

● Start with offensive players stationary and slowly passing the ball to each other. Watch for defenders' stance, reactions and footwork.

● Offensive players have to stay in their area but now they pass the ball rapidly to each other and may go one-on-one trying to drive to the basket. Defensive players must now react quickly, play one-on-one defence and be ready to help team-mates if they are beaten one-on-one.

● Guards O1 and O2 use their side of the floor to run pick and rolls with O3 and O4 or pass to them and cut to the basket. The defensive players must defend the pick and roll or jump to the ball and beat the cutter down the lane.

● Use weakside picks O3 and O4, O2 and O4. Defenders must talk and open up while seeing their opponent and the ball.

● Build up to four-on-four basketball, letting all the offensive players do what they want. Defenders must use all rules with the man-to-man defence plus rotating to help each other as shown in the second diagram. This diagram shows players' rotation for a baseline drive.

Five-on-five

This drill is competitive and uses all the skills acquired for defence in a controlled setting.

Team O has the ball on offence at half court and they may run any offence they choose. Team D plays man-to-man defence and will fast break once they have possession of the ball through steals, rebounds, or team O's field goal.

The team must work on their transition game by getting back into a half-court man-to-man defence on the missed shot or a full court man-

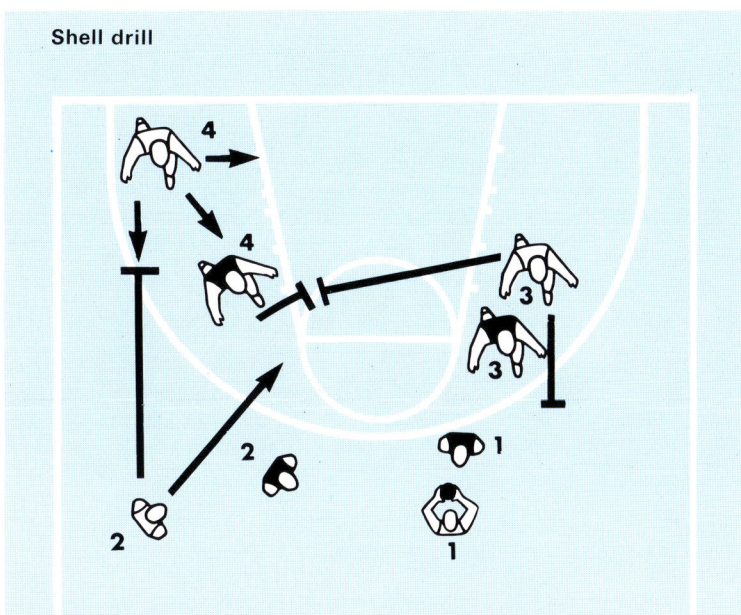

Shell drill

to-man on their successful shots. It makes no difference to team D who just push the ball down the floor and take a shot whether their shot is made or not off the fast break.

Team D then gets a chance at half court offence. That means team O has just had an offence, came back to protect against the fast break when they had to play against half-court offence.

Keep playing this way up to seven points, using your own scoring criteria such as two points for a defensive rebound, two points for taking a charge, one point for a steal, two points deducted for being scored against, one point deducted for a foul or for not calling out a pick.

Shell drill
A step-by-step drill building up from passes between stationary players to four-on-four basketball

Shell rotation drill
The defenders must help each other by rotating their defensive positions to cover a baseline drive

---

MAN-TO-MAN DEFENCE CHECKLIST

● **Be ready**, *feet spread, up on the balls of your feet and ready to move*

● **Knees bent** *to help balance and readiness to move*

● **Keep low** *keep your backside low and your back straight*

● **Head up** *and keep your eyes glued to your opponent's midriff where he will be holding the ball*

● **Arms out**, *slightly bent at the elbow, palms upwards ready to flick the ball out of your opponents hands. Don't* chop *downwards because you will foul*

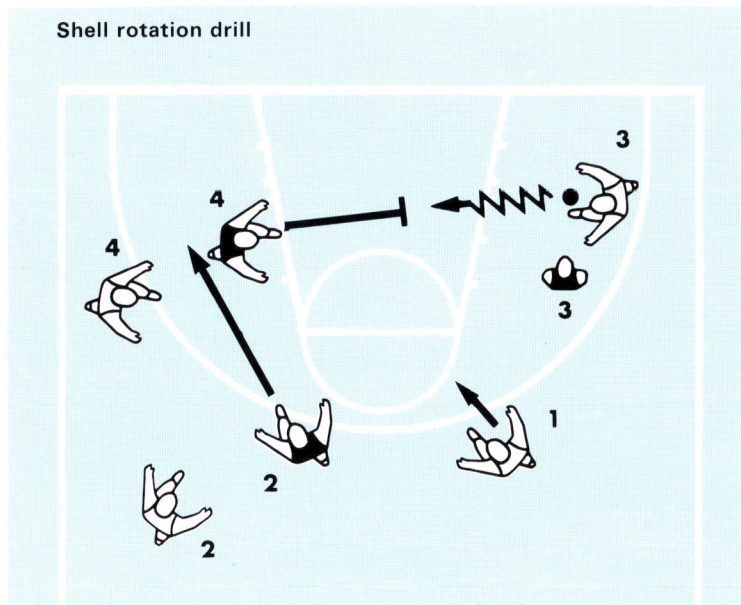

Shell rotation drill

ZONE DEFENCE

Introduction

When a coach claims that his team play man-to-man defence all the time and that teams which play zone defence are lazy, it usually means that he doesn't teach the zone defence properly. A zone defence is where you guard an area of the floor and any offensive player who enters that zone, whereas in 'man' defence you have to follow a particular offensive player all over the floor. Just because you're guarding an area of the floor, don't think it will be easy. Any player of mine who thought that zone defence was the chance to have a rest soon found out otherwise.

Zone defences are good at forcing offensive teams to play to their weaknesses. Teams with tall, powerful players can be kept away from the basket and stopped from scoring at close range, thereby forcing the team to shoot from mid or long range. Quick ball-handlers can be stopped from penetrating the defence.

When the zone defence is used over the whole court to pressure opponents, called a full court press, they can be harassed and forced into panicky mistakes. The trick is to decide which zone suits your team and, just as importantly, to decide which zone to use and against which sort of opposition.

As with everything else in basketball, the important point is how you execute. Although the professional NBA bans zone defences, every team that I have seen plays some form of zone defence at some time or another.

A defensive team may use a zone because they are slow or because they want to shield a particularly weak defensive player, but for whatever reason a zone is not an easy way out for defensive players and they'll have to work very hard to make it work effectively. Players must get out of their minds the myth that using a zone is a chance to take a breather.

A 3-2 zone formation
This formation is one of many zone defences used in basketball, where the defensive players guard a particular area of the floor and any players who move into their area

Opposite: Having a tall player at the front of your defence can make it hard for players to shoot over the defence, as James Worthy finds out against 7 ft 6 in (2.3 m) Manute Bol

3-2 zone formation

1-2-1-1 full court zone press 1

1-2-1-1 full court zone press 2

1 and 2 You don't have to start playing defence under your own basket. With a full-court zone press you begin defence almost under the other team's basket, as soon as they try to put the ball into play. This zone pressures the opponent with the ball out of bounds. When he makes a pass, the receiver can immediately be double-teamed, here by D1 and D4

1-2-1-1

This puts pressure on the inbound passer and the players first receiving the ball. It is vulnerable to an immediate pass to the half-court area and is not effective unless the number 5 man, the player guarding his own basket, can block shots.

Player 4 is usually a fairly quick forward and more importantly, has long arms. His role is to get right up on the opponent putting the ball inbounds, his arms outstretched and waving continuously. Any deflection he gets should be rewarded with a score. If the first pass is made to the attacker in front of D1 or D2, D4 immediately drops back to double team the opponent with the ball. Alternatively, he sprints down the middle of the floor, looking to intercept passes.

Player D lines up to the left of D4 around the foul line-extended area or next to the closest opponent in his area. He is usually the smaller of the two guards. He must try to stop the first pass being made to his offensive player, allowing a pass only into the corner which is the ideal place to double team an opponent with D4.

D2 is the taller of the two guards. He lines up on the opposite side from D1. The taller guard must be here because most teams inbound the ball into the opposite side, which means D2 will be left blocking the pass to the middle in which

taller offensive players have taken up position. D1 and D2 have the same roles: if the ball is inbounded on their side they double team with D4, if inbounded on the opposite side they stop the pass to the middle or top of the key area.

D3 must be your best athlete and have a sense for the ball. He must anticipate and pick off passes. If the ball goes over the heads of D1 or D2, he is there to double team the ball with either D1 or D2 who drop back. He must be a gambler, but one who wins most of the time.

D5 will usually be your tallest player, one who ideally will scare off one-on-one or two-on-one fast breaks from the opposition. He will start out as close to the half court as possible. If there is no-one behind him he will come up to the mid-court line. He must tell D3 of anyone flashing to the ball behind him and must also try to intercept the long pass to the corners. He must be absolutely certain he will intercept the pass, otherwise the basket will be unguarded. He is the last line of defence.

The idea of the press is to disrupt the player making the inbounds pass with D4 pressuring him. Let the passes in only where you want them, preferably the corners where either D4 and D1 or D4 and D2 can put on extreme pressure by double-teaming the ball while D3 tries to pick off the intermediate pass and D5 the lay-up pass.

‘ A quick team can give the appearance that they have seven or eight players on court instead of five ’

Half-court zone press

The half-court zone press has the same rules as the full-court press, used in the smaller area. This will obviously help slower teams who lack the agility and speed to press over the full court. An advantage of the half-court zone press is the element of surprise as teams usually don't spend much practice time working against half-court

zones. Again there is the strong possibility that the constant pressure may force your opponents to attempt to score in a hurry, thereby turning over possession to your defence.

Its plainest disadvantage is that a team of good ball-handlers and passers can open easy scoring opportunities.

1-3-1 half-court zone

My teams have used this press with great success. It is very important to have the right personnel for this defence.

D1 needs to be a quick guard with long arms which will discourage the other team's guards passing to each other.

D2 should be another guard who compensates for a slight lack of speed with extra size and strength to block out, because he becomes a rebounder on the weak side (away from the ball).

D3 is the key player, with above-average speed and a good awareness in anticipating the ball. He directs the defence from the back of the zone. He mustn't be afraid to stand his ground and take a charge from a player running at the basket, since the offensive team may penetrate the zone.

D4 is usually a rebounding forward. Since most teams favour the right side of the floor he must have good court sense to protect the basket from the lob pass aimed at a player running in on the 'blind side'.

D5 is the forward-centre type who must be very active with above average speed to stop the ball in the middle and also to sprint to cover the low post when the ball is moved to the corner. If you have no player who can do this, think about playing a different defence! There are bound to be holes in the defence and you will need a tall player to block them.

Trapping areas

The first diagram shows players' initial positions and areas on the floor that are good to trap opponents with the ball.

Just over half court and in the corners are better areas to double-team the ball than the inter-mediate wing area.

Slides

D1 must push the ball-handler to one side of the floor and not let him dribble back. This will help D4 and D2 recognize their areas. If the ball is pushed towards D2, D4 moves back to protect the basket and vice versa. All players should have their arms spread at all times taking up as much of the passing lanes as possible. They raise their arms overhead only when double-teaming the ball.

Since the corners appear to offer safe passes for the offence, the defensive slides for when the ball is in the corner are illustrated. Note that D1 can stop the passes to the high post or wing, while D4 can either guard the left wing if D1 has the high post or stop the pass to the high post if D1 denies the wing.

Half-court zone press
These are the danger areas for the team with the ball when you're playing a half-court zone press. The shaded 'trap' areas are the best places to double-team the player with the ball, especially at the halfway line and in the corners

Half court zone press

1-3-1 half-court zone slide
D3 cuts out the baseline drive; D2 attacks the ball in the corner, blocking the passing lane; D4 moves into the lane or to the high post position; D5 takes the low post and fronts the offensive player; D1 either goes to the high post or gambles on a pass back to the wing vacated by D2

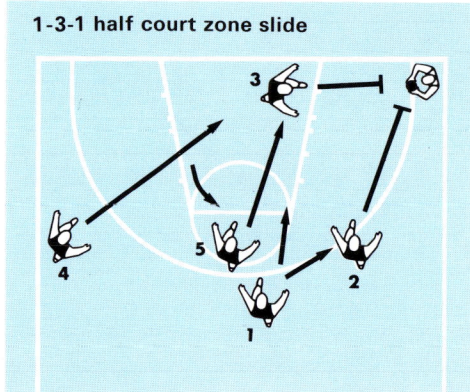

1-3-1 half court zone slide

2-3 and 2-1-2 zone defences

The 2-3 and the 2-1-2 are the most frequently used zones in basketball. From school level to the top teams you will find they all use the zones with two players at the front. These are called even front zones, meaning two players at the top of the zone; the odd front has one player up top as in the 1-3-1 or the 1-2-2 zone defence.

Both the 2-3 and the 2-1-2 are popular because they are easy to teach and can be played by just about anybody. You don't need exceptional athletes or height to play these zones. If you're smart and if you hustle, the even front zones may help your team.

The difference between a 2-3 and a 2-1-2 zone depends on who you have covering the wings: in a 2-3 the low men or forwards cover the wings and in a 2-1-2 the guards hustle and cover the wings.

Players need particular abilities for the even-front zones.

D1 and D2 have to be quick and, especially in the 2-1-2, have to cover a large area. They can't slack or the zone will crumble.

D3 and D4 must both have some speed to be able to cover the corners if the opposition have a player who can shoot accurately from there. Since more shots are said to be taken on the right side of the floor put the best rebounder of the two on the left of the basket as this is where missed shots are most likely to fall.

D5 should be the tallest, broadest player, one who can take up a lot of space inside, under the basket. He must know how to guard the low and the high post and be able to rebound in a crowd of players.

Slides

The diagrams show the different coverage of the pass to the wing. The first diagram shows the 2-1-2 formation with the guard D1 covering the wing and the second the 2-3 alignment with the forward D3 covering the wing.

The 2-3 can also be used to trap. The element of surprise, plus the quality of the double team are the keys.

The third diagram shows the trap as the ballhandler just crosses the half-court line. D1 and D2 spring out and attack the ball with their hands raised, setting a good double team. D3 and D4 rush out into the passing lanes ready to intercept a pass. D5 stands in front of any opponent in the middle.

The fourth diagram shows how to trap out of the 2-3 when the ball is in the corner. D4 rushes out under control to trap with D2, who cuts off the passing lane while attacking the ball. D1 denies the pass back to the wing area, D3 denies high post and D5 fronts the low post.

2-1-2 zone wing coverage

2-3 zone wing coverage

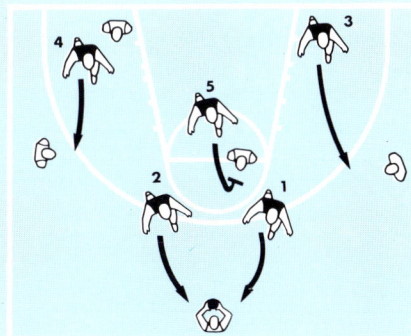
2-3 trap

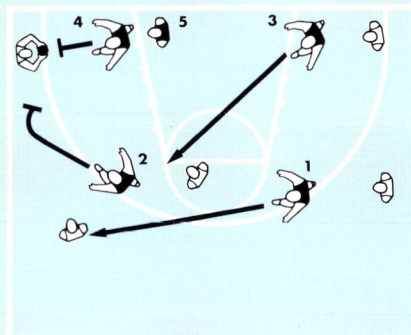
2-3 trap in corner

2-3 and 2-1-2 zone defences
These defences are easy to learn and can be played at every level. You don't have to be tall or a super athlete, but if you work hard and hustle you can make these zones a success

2-1-2 zone wing coverage
The zone is under threat from a player on the wing with the ball

2-3 zone wing coverage
The zone moves across to cover the player with the ball on the wing

2-3 trap
The 3-2 zone is springing into a surprise trap with D1 and D2 moving up to attack the ball-handler, D3 and D4 attack the passing lanes and D5 is ready to block any player in the middle

2-3 trap in corner
Another trap springing out of the 3-2 zone, this time when the ballhandler is in the corner

3-2 zone

3-2 zone is excellent for teams that use three smaller players with two bigger ones. This allows the smaller players to spread their coverage while the big ones stay closer to the basket. One problem is weakside rebounding which may fall to a guard. The basic 3-2 set is shown in the first diagram.

D1 is a point guard who is quick, one you would want handling the ball if you were running a fast break. He doesn't move out further than the top of the key unless the offensive team have an accurate three-point shooter.

3-2 zone formation
1 The three shorter players are away from the basket and the two taller players close to the basket

2 The two taller players are sliding across to cover the ball in the corner, supported by D1

3 The ball-handler is at the high post. D4 and D5 converge on him with D1, while D2 and D3 rotate

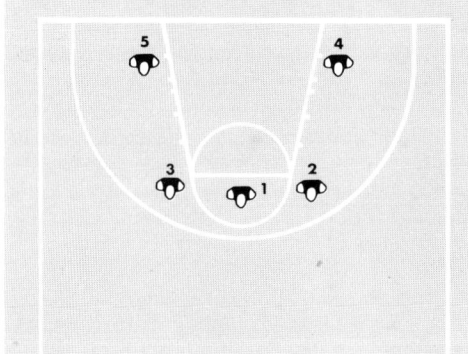

3-2 zone formation 1

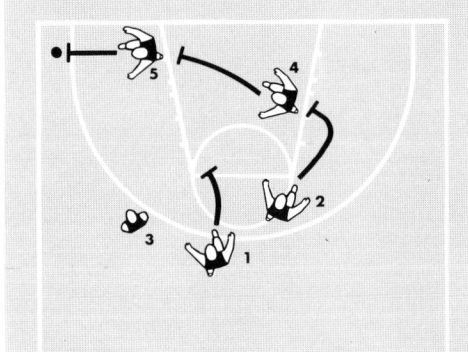

3-2 zone formation 2

3-2 zone formation 3

D2 is on the left wing; since most teams like to start on the right side he should be the better defender. He must be able to rebound and quickly get out on the fast break.

D3 on the right wing must be a good rebounder as more shots will come from the right side of the floor and therefore drop onto his side of the floor.

D2 and D3 start with their inside foot where the foul line and the edge of the key meet.

D4 is the rear man on the left side, the quicker of the two rear men as he will probably have to cover the corner more often.

D5 is the rear man on the right side, the strongest player and best rebounder who must be able to play the post and the corner and still rebound.

D4 and D5 start out with one foot in the lane and as high as possible (that is as far from the basket as possible) as the offence lets them.

Slides

The second diagram shows the 3-2 slides, or team movements, for when the ball is in the corner.

D5 goes out to the corner under control. D4 fronts the low post. D3 protects the medium post area (in between high and low). D1 helps cover the high post. D2 is the weakside rebounder.

The third diagram shows what happens when the ball is at the high post.

D5 moves up to play the high post. D4 protects against the high to low pass. D2 and D3 protects the baseline. D1 doubles the high post.

1-3-1 zone

The 1-3-1 zone defence can be used as a basic zone or a trapping zone. It can cause the offence difficulties because it spreads out the offence and it may therefore require longer passes to penetrate the zone. It also keeps a good rebounding team further away from the basket especially at the guard and small forward positions.

Weaknesses depend on the individuals playing the zone. The baseline player is the key, since he has low post coverage initially and must also be a rebounder, move out quickly to the corners and direct others from the back. Although 1-3-1 is a team defence it puts a lot of pressure on one player. So before you decide on playing a 1-3-1 zone make sure you have a baseline player on the team.

Players

D1 is a quick guard who must lead the fast break. Depending on the offensive threats of the guards he may initially start at the top of the key or as far as 5 ft (1.5 m) past the three-point line.

D2 left wing is a good defensive player who can rebound, usually your off guard.

1-3-1 zone formation 1

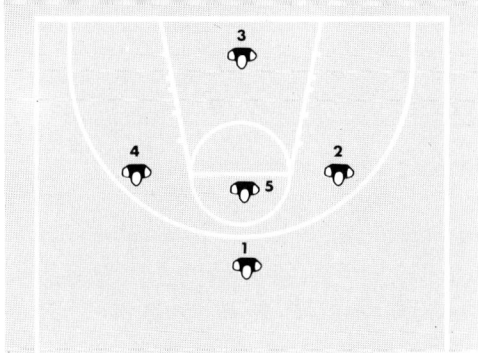

1-3-1 zone formation 2

D4 right wing should be the second best rebounder and a player with some extra size but he must not be slow.

D2 and D4 start at the foul line extended area, not letting any player start inside, basket-side of them.

D5 middle should be the best rebounder who must deny the pass into the high post and front the low post.

The ball must be kept out of the middle of the floor in a 1-3-1 zone defence, so this player is very important. He starts around the foul line or wherever the nearest offensive player is to that position.

D3-back is the most important player in the zone.

He must be a good athlete because he has to do so much: cover the corners, front the low post, rebound and direct the others.

Slides

The first diagram shows the initial formation. The second shows the most difficult slide when the ball goes in the corner.

D3 goes to the corner under control and doesn't let his opponent go along the baseline. D5 covers the low post by fronting the offensive player. D1 covers the high post. D2 gives help to D3 in case his offensive player drives at the basket. D4 is a weakside rebounder (away from the ball).

Match-up zone

The match-up is a zone played with man-to-man principles. You don't just play an area as in a basic zone, you play the man in your area man-to-man. A team must be a sound man-to-man team to play an effective match-up.

The advantages in playing a match-up are that you:
● may confuse your opponent: teams have trouble recognizing what defence you are in. They don't know whether to run their zone offence (that is against a zone defence) or their man-to-man offence (against a man-to-man defence).
● cut down screening effectiveness. Since you're not playing basic man-to-man, teams can't use screens as effectively as they would against a man defence. Remember you're playing whichever player enters your area, not a particular player wherever he goes. If a defender is beaten by the dribbler the other four players are still playing their zones, so the dribbler will drive smack into a zone. The match-up also allows a team to sag away from certain players and deny others the ball. This will help you to try and expose a team's weaknesses.

The disadvantages in playing a match-up are:
● mismatches. If your rebounders are shorter you will have trouble, since because you have individual match-ups a taller team can take advantage.
● difficulty in learning. Match-up can also prove difficult for some certain players to grasp. There are different match-up zones and I will briefly explain one. The first was originated by a coach called Bill Green who coached the successful Marion High School, Indiana, programme and then became head coach of the University of Indiana at Indianapolis. His match-up is based on a numerical system, with each defender having a number and specific rules to go with it. Firstly the team shows a basic team alignment on the first offence and then begins to match-up. The first diagram demonstrates players and positions.

D1 is a quick, sound ball-handler, handles the fast break, always applies pressure to whoever he is guarding. The rule for D1 is to force the point man on offence, with or without the ball, to his right. The point man holds the central position in the offensive team's alignment usually at the top of the key. When he is the ball-handler he is known as the point guard.

D2 must be prepared to play against taller players. He will have to rebound on the weakside and must be quick and strong and must block out. The rules for D2 are to take the first player to D1's left.

D3 is a forward and probably the weakest defensive player. He must block out and rebound. D3 takes the first player to D1's right.

1-3-1 zone formation
1 This zone makes the offence spread out and can force them to use longer passes, which are more likely to be intercepted

2 D3 is the key player in the 1-3-1. As the zone slides to cover the ball in the corner, for example, D3 has to cover the corners, front the low post and direct the other defenders from his position at the rear of the zone

Match-up zones
The players and positions in a match-up zone out of an initial 3-2 alignment

Match-up zone

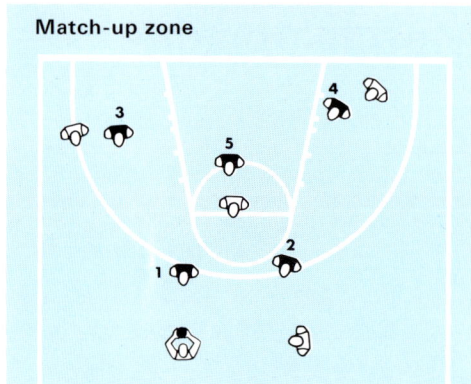

Match-up for a 1-4 zone
D1 is at the front of the zone, close up to the guard with the ball

Match-up for a 1-4 zone

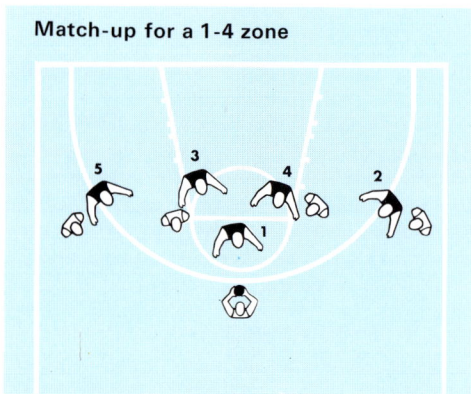

Match-up overload
The overload is when three or more of the offensive team take to one side of the floor

Match-up overload

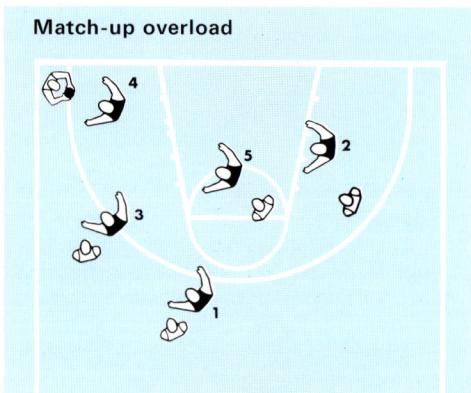

Match-up cutter
The cutter, who was initially guarded by D2, cuts through the defence and is picked up by D3, leaving the other defensive players to adjust as the other offensive players rotate their positions

Match-up cutter

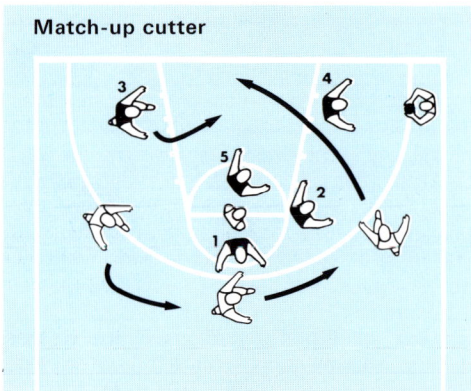

D4 is the key player and must be quick, intelligent and tall. He takes the second player to the right or left of the point man.

D5 is the centre, your best rebounder. He takes the post. If there is no high post player D5 plays the right low post position.

The second diagram shows the match-up for a 1-4 zone defence. D1 guards the point, D2 takes first player to D1's left, D3 takes first player to D1's right, D5 takes high post to the right, D4 takes high post to the left.

The third diagram shows how to defend the overload zone offence. The rule applies that D4 takes the second player to the right or left of the point.

The fourth diagram shows the match-up versus the cutter. D2's opponent cuts through the offence and is picked up by D3. D1's opponent rotates so D2 picks him up, with D1 picking up D3's player who has rotated to the point.

Junk defences

Junk defences are tactics that do not fit into the more common zone defences. They are used for various reasons. For example the defensive team may be inferior and feel they need to try and confuse the opposition, the opponents may have only two players who do all the scoring or defenders may prefer these defences to playing man-to-man.

My teams have used both the triangle-and-two and the box-and-one defences when we felt that we couldn't match-up well enough with our personnel. In some games when we just couldn't stop certain players from scoring, we found more success with either the triangle or the box. A good scorer will get his points somehow, but a player who needs to shoot from a long way out to score can be bothered by these defences.

Just like any other defences, the more you work the better you will become. The same holds true for the box and the triangle. It will be difficult to expect your team to execute these defences well without good practice time. My teams will work a little on these defences during the course of the year so when you have two or three days to prepare for a game and you want to use these defences put on extra time to familiarize the team.

Box-and-one defence
The diagram shows this defence in its initial alignment. It consists of four players playing a 2-2 zone or box while one player, D3, is face-guarding the designated offensive player: his job is to prevent his opponent getting the ball. If he does get the ball, D3's job is to force him to the next nearest defenders so they can double team him. D3 must be a tough, durable player as the opposition may try anything to get their player free. The players in the box zone play their

positions as if in a 3-2 zone (page 68). The second diagram shows their slides when the ball is in the corner. The 3-2 slides put D4 out on the ball, D5 fronting the low post, D1 as weakside rebounder and D2 covering the high post.

The third diagram shows the box defending the high post when he has the ball. D5 becomes the up man up to the high post area and plays the post man-to-man, D4 covers baseline and D1 and D2 are ready to cover the next pass to the wings.

This can be an effective defence when you know your opponents very well. There are many disadvantages such as being open to penetration from the top and wings, rebounding, quick ball movement and covering outside shooters. I suggest that younger teams spend their time working on basic man-to-man or zones rather than on the box-and-one. But if you have the time and you're happy with your team's progress on fundamental defences then it's a good one to have up your sleeve.

Triangle-and-two defence

This defence is used primarily when the offensive team have two players they rely on to do the bulk of their scoring. Coaching in Europe has led me to use this defence more than I thought I ever would, since most European countries allow two foreign players per team and these players, usually Americans, are relied on to do most of the scoring. This may be because the coach thinks it's the best way to win games or the foreign player may feel he has to live up to his big contract. Whatever the reason, we may use the triangle-and-two in these cases.

The first diagram shows the triangle-and-two defence as the offence set up ready to attack. D3 has one of the jobs of stopping his opponent from getting the ball. This is because your number 3 player is usually your best athlete. D1 has the other job, he has to be quick and not easily intimidated since he may be facing a taller player. D2 is at the point of the triangle, and should be your off guard who has speed, size, and can rebound. D4 and D5 are your tallest players and the best rebounders.

A team shouldn't run the triangle-and-two defence if the opposition has more than two outstanding perimeter shooters as the two defenders will be outnumbered. But if they have only two this allows the triangle to sag away from the offensive players and protect the middle.

1-1-3 zone defence

This zone can be used when the opposition guards are weak ball-handlers and/or don't quickly see which style of defence their opponents are playing. The 1-1-3 will allow you to put man-to-man pressure on the guards and also disguises your 2-3 zone defence.

The first diagram shows the initial alignment. The guards D1 and D2 can pressurize the offensive guards by double teaming, running and

Junk defence box-and-one defence 1

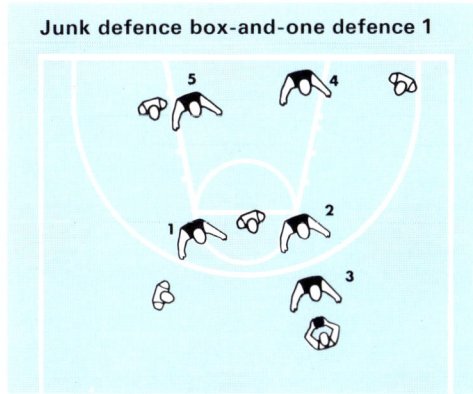

Junk defence box-and-one defence 2

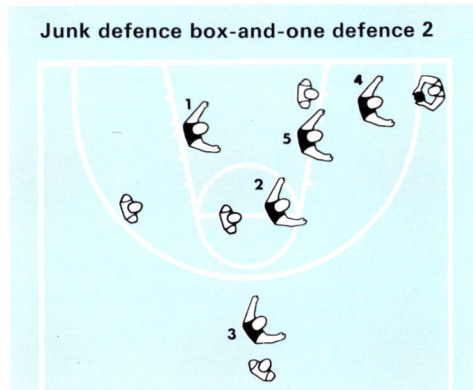

Junk defence box-and-one defence 3

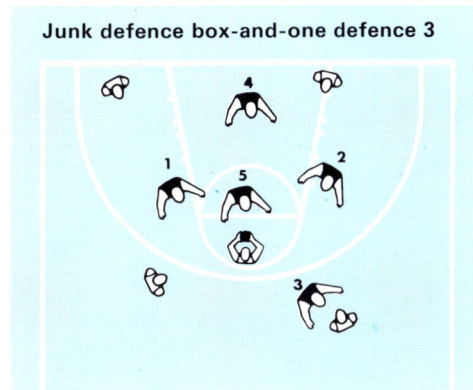

Junk defence triangle-and-two defence

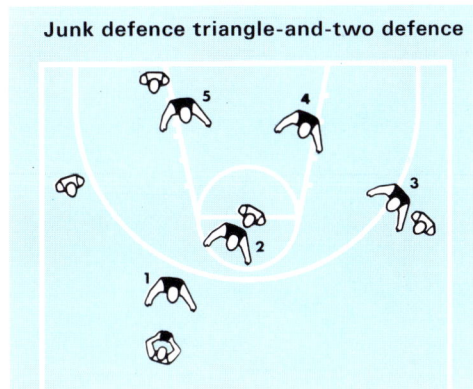

Junk defence box-and-one
1 Four players are in a 2-2 zone with the one free player ready to follow his opponent wherever he goes

2 When the ball is moved to the corner the four players in the box slide to cover the threat from that area

3 When the ball is at the high post, D3 is still keeping his opponent out of the action, while the box moves up to defend against the ball-handler on the foul line

Junk defence triangle-and-two
D3 is trying to stop his player from getting the ball, D1 is guarding the dribbler while the other three defenders sag away to protect the middle of their defence

1-1-3 zone defence
1 D1 and D2 are pressuring the guards and ready to double-team the player with the ball

2 The offence are now in your half of the court and you have to be ready to adapt and adjust. When the passer moves the ball out to the wing D1, who was guarding the ball-handler, drops back to his position in the 2-3 zone. D2 guards the player who has the ball

2-2-1 zone press
The 'Blue Game' plan: the basic alignment for the zone press, which we reverted to, after scoring a field basket

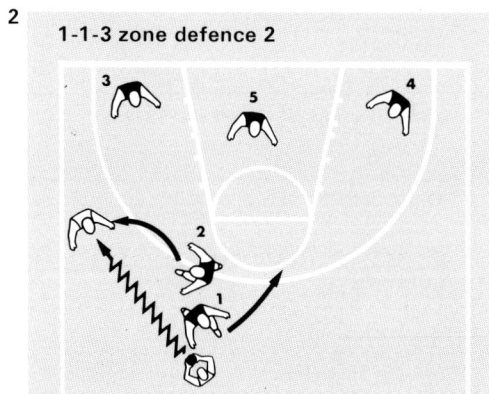

1

1-1-3 zone defence 1

2-2-1 zone press

2

1-1-3 zone defence 2

jumping or by just playing aggressive man-to-man defence. D1 must put extreme pressure on the ball-handler and make him turn his back on his team-mate. D3, D4 and D5 are back on defence as in a 2-3 zone with D3 ready to intercept passes.

The second diagram shows what happens when the offence crosses half court and passes the ball. D2 takes the first pass to the wing and D1 falls back into his 2-3 zone position. D3, D4 and D5 are now playing basic 2-3 zone.

The 1-1-3 won't work against a team that fast breaks efficiently as there won't be enough time for D1 and D2 to apply pressure. It may work against a team that walks the ball up the floor especially if their guards aren't confident.

Changing defences

In the early 1980s a popular game strategy was to change defences numerous time during the course of the game. The exceptional athletes playing basketball meant that simply playing basic man-to-man and zone defence wasn't good enough. The players on offence were still dominating. The changing of defences is not just for appearances. You design your changes to suit the personnel you have. There are various reasons for using changing defences.

● To control the tempo to suit your team. Since a team can win a match with a run of 10 to 15 consecutive points, coaches are very wary that their opponents don't get away from them. Changing defences may help speed up or slow down a game to suit a team's strengths.
● To expose weaknesses in the opposition. If you

1-2-1-1 zone press

1-3-1 half-court trap

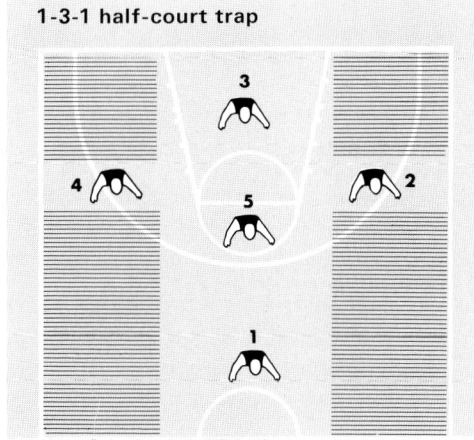

1-2-1-1 zone press
It is a good moment to put on a 1-2-1-1 zone press after scoring from a free throw because you can be ready in position while the free throws are being taken

1-3-1 half-court trap
These are the ideal 'trapping' areas where you should try to double-team the player with the ball

scout a team well and if you use your practice time to prepare specifically for particular opponents you can change defences to take away your opponents' strengths. For example, if a team has only two good perimeter shooters and one of them is on the bench to rest or in foul trouble, you may want to concentrate for a few minutes on the other shooter. Another example may be that a team is resting their point guard. This may be a good chance to employ a full-court press to rattle his back-up player.
● Players like changing defences. If players enjoy their game they'll play better.

Game plan

Team with four small and one tall player

A team with this line-up will often be classed as underdogs, but that will often make them very exciting to coach and a very exciting team in which to be a player. These players will have to push themselves to the limit when playing defence but if they are prepared to do that, they will be very successful. A team with just one tall

player will be pounded on their own defensive boards if they sit back in a static half-court zone defence. So they must use the extra speed and quickness of their smaller players, by taking the defence to their opponents and by being prepared to play defence all over the court.

One season I had a small team and we had a losing run because we sat back on defence and allowed the offence to dictate the play. But when we switched to what I called our 'Blue Game' we had 20 consecutive wins, stayed unbeaten until the end of the season and won the National League Championship in England.

This was how the 'Blue Game' worked:
● After we scored a field basket from open play we immediately formed up in a 2-2-1 full court zone press, then changed into a 2-3 match-up zone when we were back in our own half. This was very confusing for our opponents because no sooner had they realized we were in a 2-2-1 and beat it, we changed into a new defence.
● After we missed a field basket and the ball remained 'live' we would immediately pick up on the offensive players by using a man-to-man defence.
● After we scored from a free throw we went into a 1-2-1-1 full court zone press.
● After we missed from a free throw we used a half-court man-to-man defence.
● When our opponents put the ball into play at the sideline we used a 1-3-1 half-court trap to trap the ball-handler.

This pressure defence wore down our opponents and it can do the same for the team you play in. When we had the ball we ran at the defence at every opportunity, so our offence became a continuation of our all-action defence. We scored from 55 per cent of our shots, averaged 98 points per game and we won over half the matches despite trailing at half-time, which underlines how we wore down our opponents.

This 'Blue Plan' fits into the philsophy of playing man-to-man defence at every opportunity, because we missed roughly half of our shots and we played 'man' every time we missed.

INDIVIDUAL MOVES

Introduction

I can't emphasize too strongly how important footwork is. When players have mastered proper footwork involving pivoting, and making jump stops and fakes while staying always under control they'll find basketball easier to play.

There are numerous times during the course of the game where improper footwork leads to a turnover or loss of possession through such violations as travelling or an illegal dribble. Poor footwork can also lose a player a good scoring opportunity, for example through poor pivoting.

One of the basic moves, stepping across the defensive player to keep him away from the ball

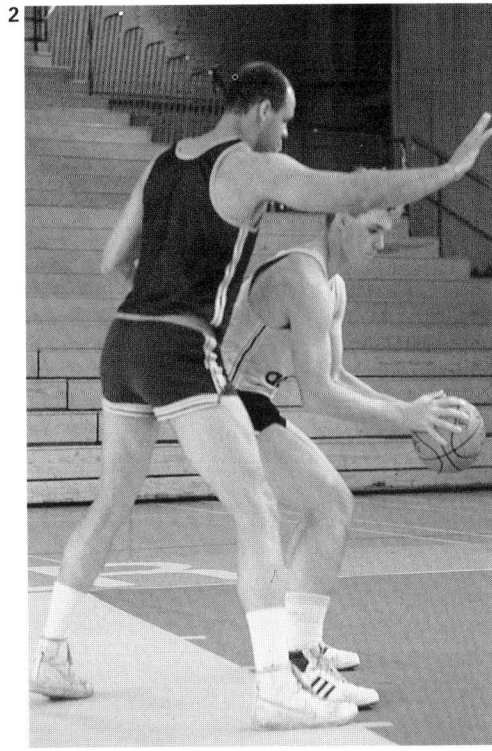

1 and 2
A player with his back to the basket and a defender behind him uses the pivot to make room

Opposite: The triple threat position gives a player the correct stance to attack the defence

Magic Johnson of the Los Angeles Lakers has the ball and now he, his opponents and the crowd are waiting for his next move. A player must make something happen to help his team. You must try to shoot, to pass or to dribble

basket, faking one way while drop-stepping the other way to obtain an inside position. They can also square up, fake a shot and step past the defender for a shot from inside their opponent.

Guards and forwards should practise the cross-over steps and rocker steps explained later (page 81). Forwards should also practise specific skills at the wing area. If they are closely guarded when they receive the ball they should turn inwards towards the basket by pivoting on their inside foot and square up to the basket. From this position they can use cross-over and rocker steps to beat their opponent. If they are closely guarded they can perform a rear pivot and step past their defender, creating a space for the baseline drive.

In possession of the ball

You've worked hard at the defensive end of the floor and you've sprinted down the court on offence, worked hard again to get open for a pass and now at last you've just received the ball. What next?

The first thing to do is to recognize if you're open enough to shoot the ball. If you are, you must determine whether you're in your shooting range. This range differs for every player; some players can shoot comfortably from 25 ft (8 m) away while others can't from as close as 10 ft (3 m)! Players that make the most of their shots immediately recognize whether or not they are within their shooting range.

If you're out of range try to pass the ball to an open team-mate closer to the basket.

If you've no shot 'on' and can't find an open team-mate, try and take the ball closer to the basket yourself, by making fakes or dribble moves to penetrate the defence and either shoot or create a scoring chance for one of your team-mates.

If all three options are unavailable, pass the ball back out to the playmaker on the perimeter of your offence and make something happen off the ball by cutting to the basketball or screening for someone else.

These four moves can't be made without putting yourself in the ideal stance to make things happen. This is the triple threat position.

Triple threat position
This stance is similar to the man-to-man defensive stance (page 52) with the difference that the player has the ball. It is called the triple threat position because the player can shoot, pass or dribble from this one position.

The player receives the ball and faces the basket standing on the balls of his feet, which are a little more than a shoulder's width apart, with the knees bent, back upright, shoulders square to the basket, head up and eyes on the basket. The hands should hold the ball in a position to shoot. This stance gives a player the proper balance necessary for attacking the defensive player.

Remember the offensive player with the ball has the advantage since he can make so many things happen. The defensive player has to react while the offensive player can act. This action can't be as effective if the player is off balance or has his back to the basket. Of course there are times when players are further away from the basket and must hold the ball overhead while trying to make a pass. Or, they're being pressured defensively so much that they must protect the ball. Nevertheless they should still strive to be an offensive threat by adopting the triple threat position to put the defender on the defensive!

You have the ball and now you must make something happen to help your team

1

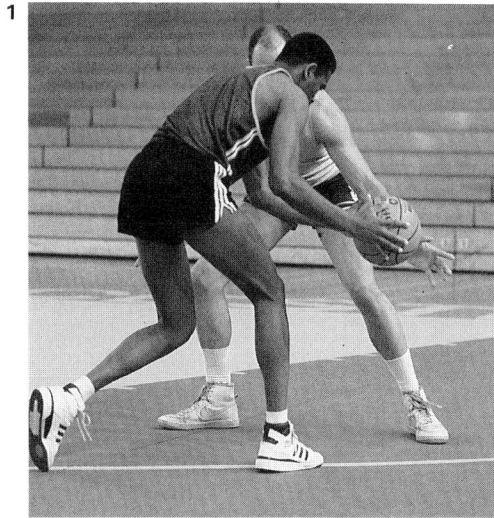

One-on-one moves

Although basketball is certainly a team game it is also broken down into individual match-ups, offensively and defensively, between particular pairs or groups of players. A team may execute an offence to get a player open for a shot and that player must utilize his 1-on-1; make an instant decision based on what the defender is doing.

● If a defender is sagging you (holding off and playing away from you) think about taking a jump shot

● Check and see if the defender is balanced, and if not act quickly before he recovers his correct position and stance

● If his knees aren't bent in a good defensive stance, attack him, because he isn't ready to play defence

Ball fake

1 The ball-handler fakes a move to the right

2 Now he draws back and appears to attempt a shot, forcing the defender to stand up straight

3 With the defender committed to blocking a shot, the dribbler moves past him

2

3

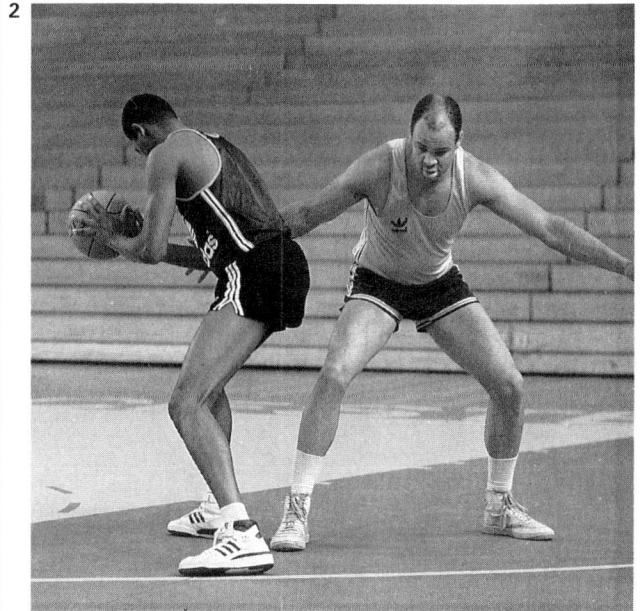

● Fake a shot or a pass to see if he over-reacts and commits himself

● If the defender is crowding you think about attacking the basket immediately, which may draw contact and result in a foul being called against the defender.

These five points will help an offensive player make his initial decision but you'll need more than that to beat a good defensive player. Here are some answers that you can work on by yourself.

Ball fake

This is moving the ball around as in a fake pass, fake dribble or a fake shot, known as a pump fake. A fake pass or dribble is used to create some room or to get the defender off balance by lunging one way or the other.

The pump fake is used to get the defender off his feet and jumping to block the anticipated shot, when you can then drive past him or draw a foul. When using a pump fake you must look at the basket to convince a defender you're going to shoot, using a quick fake with the ball as if to shoot while snapping your head up. This head fake while showing the ball should make the defender react.

Catch and shoot

A good time to attack the defender is the moment you first receive the ball. Often the defender won't expect you to shoot so suddenly and won't be in a good defensive stance.

Catch and go

Once you receive the ball put your non-dribbling shoulder down and dribble towards the basket. Always have your body between the ball and the defender. This quick move will catch the defender off balance and will help to draw a foul.

Jab step

This jab or half step will make the defender retreat and free you for a jump shot. While facing your defender in a triple threat position you jab a hard half step to one side of the defender towards the basket. This can be combined with a ball fake as if to dribble. If the defender retreats from the jab step and then is starting to recover use a pump fake and drive past the defender.

Rocker step

The offensive player steps towards the defender then rocks back as if to assume his initial position. As the defender leans forward again the offensive player pushes off with his back foot and explodes past the defender.

Crossover step

This starts with a jab step to one side of the detender, getting the detender to lean that way, but the offensive player then quickly takes a big step crossing in front of the defender to his other side. This big step is accompanied by a power dribble to help you to step by the defender.

The reverse pivot

Jack Sikma, another of the stars of the NBA, has made his living out of this step, which can be used whether you're 2 ft (0.6 m) or 20 ft (6 m) away from the basket. Use it when you have your back to the basket and your back to the defender, when you have both feet on the ground and have not established a pivot foot. Turn to face the basket by pivoting on the left foot, and swing the right leg toward the defender, which will cause him to straighten up and back off a little.

You will now be in the triple threat position facing the basket, and be ready to shoot, dribble or pass the ball. Jack Sikma usually shoots the ball.

Crossover step
1 The dribbler makes a move to one side of the defender

2 Then he takes a big step across the defender to the other side

Moving without the ball

When playing basketball you should never stand still on offence. You must keep moving even when you haven't got the ball. By moving all the time, you're trying to win not only a physical contest with your opponent but also a psychological one. Constant screening, cutting and fighting for rebounding position will wear your defender down. Don't just run around without a reason but try to get yourself or a team-mate into a better scoring position.

A player can't play this type of basketball without being in good condition. You can't be a half-hearted player and move well without the ball. The more you play the better shape you will be in and the smarter you will get. When you play in games, practise or play on the playground, work hard on moving without the ball and the game will become easier.

A player must learn to play with his team-mates, to recognize the best and worst passers on the team, to know who sets the hardest screens and also not to bunch up with other players. Learn also to recognize when a team-mate is giving you a clue. Some players will nod their heads when they want you to cut to the basket so that they can pass to you. Others will wave at you to move closer to them while others will motion for you to come closer so that you can screen their man.

1-3 The offensive player makes a move in front of the defender, but then cuts behind him in a 'back door' move

Moves to get free

Back door

I believe that back door play is one of the best examples of the team work that is required for successful basketball. This play works best when a player is being overplayed or crowded by the defender. The offensive player fakes as if going to step away from the basket to receive a pass, then suddenly turns and explodes to the basket with one hand up to give the passer a target. When worked correctly this play usually results in a lay-up.

Another more exciting version is the back door lob, where the passer throws the ball up near the rim and his team-mate, who unexpectedly went back door, jumps up and either puts the ball in the basket or more convincingly dunks the ball.

V cut

This cut is used on the wing areas to free a player for a pass. The wing player is being marked closely by the defender and takes two or three steps towards the basket, then cuts sharply on an angle towards the passer. This cut initially gives the impression of a back door play but by cutting towards the ball the offensive player reduces the distance between him and the passer. The pass should always be made to the outside shoulder away from the receiver's defender.

L cut

The L cut is another way of getting free to receive

V cut

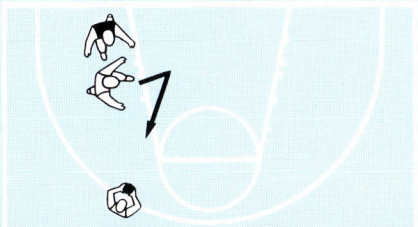

L cut

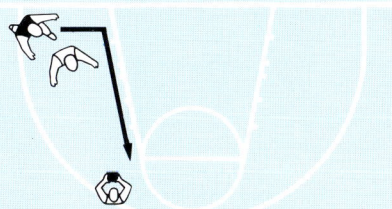

V cut
To escape for a pass when being closely guarded on the wing, make a strong move towards the basket, then cut in a 'V' back towards the passer to receive the ball

L cut
Start as if making a back-door play to the basket, then cut up the lane to receive the pass on the free-throw line

a pass. The player starts a back door cut but then darts straight up the lane to receive the pass on the free-throw line. This is useful when the defender is overplaying the offensive man and expecting a V cut.

Post cut

These are cuts made in the post area to free a player in the key area under the basket. In basketball most of the action is away from the ball. This is where the post cuts come into play. When the ball is on the wing, the post player you want to pass to will usually be on the opposite low post. To avoid a violation the post player has only three seconds to free himself and make his move while in the key area. The first rule is to fake a move towards one direction before cutting to the place where you actually want to receive the ball.

If you want the ball at the high post your initial move is a big hard step towards the low post with your foot closest to the baseline. You then spring off your foot and take a bigger step with your opposite foot towards the high post, watching the passer and getting both your hands ready to receive the pass.

If you want the ball on the low post make a long, positive step with your foot away from the baseline towards the high post and then spring off it by taking a large step with your opposite foot towards the low post. You don't want to be fronted or denied the ball so you must use your arms to get position in front of the defender. Once you have the defender on your back take up a semi-crouched position making yourself a wide target for the passer. Keep your elbows up to prevent the defender reaching round and intercepting the pass.

STAR TIP

☆If you ask defenders in the NBA what makes it so difficult to guard Larry Bird some will mention his jump shot or his rebounding. But the better defenders will say it's his knack of moving without the ball. Bird is not a great leaper nor is he super fast, so how does he get open? By reading the defence and knowing his team-mates he can predict when he'll get the ball. Basketball players have to know how to move without the ball.

Two-on-two play

The two-on-two plays used today were devised 40 years ago. There is nothing fancy about two-on-two basketball. The secret is in the execution. The reason they still work today even though the players are quicker, taller and stronger is that the plays are so difficult to defend.

Give and go
This is a basic pass and cut play to beat the defender to the basket. Offensive player O1 has the ball and passes to O2 who has freed himself for the pass. O1 then makes a jab step away from O2 and makes a strong cut towards O2 but on a line towards the basket. O1's job is to get ball side, or positioned closer to O2 to receive the pass without his defensive player deflecting the ball.

Once O2 has his defensive player on his back he gives a target by extending his outside arm for the ball. The pass should lead O1 a little towards the basket by passing slightly in front of him on the line of his run.

Pick and roll
When executed correctly the pick and roll, or screen and roll, is probably one of the easiest methods of creating scoring opportunities. It is most effective with a good shooter or penetrator holding the ball and a tall player setting the screen or pick. The screener shouldn't be afraid of contact since he will get bumped.

The screener sets a pick in an area which is in the ball-handler's shooting range. He sets a pick by having his feet in a wide stance with his arms hanging down and slightly bent. He doesn't run up to the defender but gives enough distance so the ball-handler has room to use the pick. The

Pick and roll
1 At the start of the pick and roll the dribbler makes towards his teammate who is setting a screen for the defender guarding the dribbler

2 The defender guarding the dribbler runs into the screen, while the dribbler moves towards the other defender

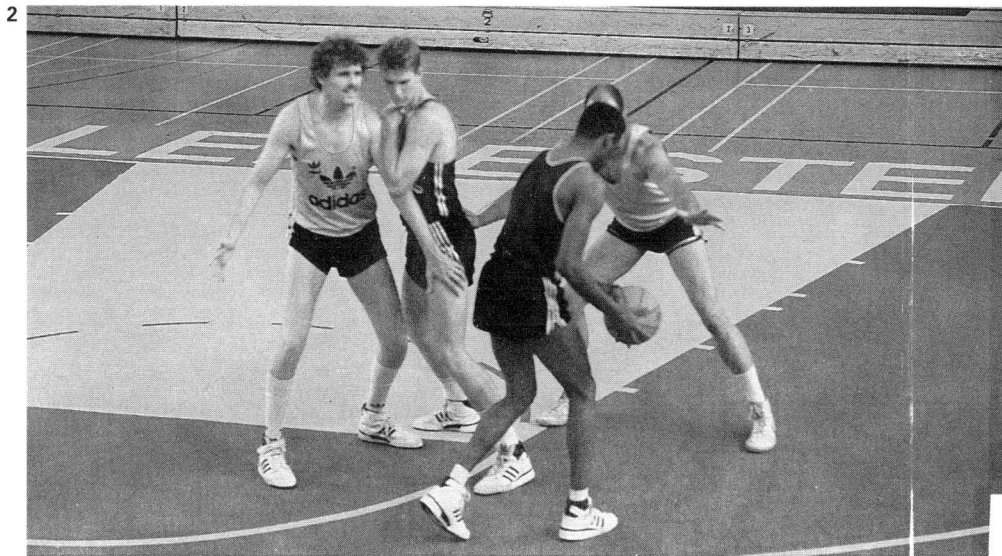

screener mustn't move his feet or swing his arms as this is a foul. The ball-handler must set his defender up by faking away from the pick first, then dribbling hard close by the pick, brushing his shoulder against the screener to prevent the defender from squeezing through. The ball-handler maintains his dribble, recognizing whether or not he has the chance for a good shot. If not, the screener pivots on his foot nearest the basket and 'rolls' towards the hoop taking a giant step with his opposite foot and never taking his eyes off the dribbler. The screener must give the dribbler a good target for the pass, having his hands out and showing where he wants to receive the ball.

Pass and go behind
This play is a version of the pick and roll.

Offensive player O1 has the ball and passes to O2 who has freed himself in the wing area. O1

takes a jab step towards the basket giving the impression that it's a give and go play, then moves towards his team-mate and goes behind him to take a hand-off pass (taking the ball off his team-mate's hand) from O2. The first option is for O1 to take his hand off and go to the basket using O2 as a screen. The second is for O2, after handing off the ball to O1, to go to the edge of the foul line and pivot on his foot closest to the basket then turn to roll to the basket catching the defender by surprise. The goal for O2 is to get his defender on his back posting up and enabling O1 to reach him with a pass.

The beauty of these moves is their simplicity. They rely on understanding between the two offensive players and crisp and quick execution of the moves. The aim is always to get one of the offensive players into the clear to shoot, pass or dribble, leaving one of the defenders left behind and out of the play for a few crucial seconds.

3 The screener now steps back from the defender and towards the basket, ready for the dribbler to pass the ball behind the other defender

4 The screener is now in the clear to take the pass and make for the basket

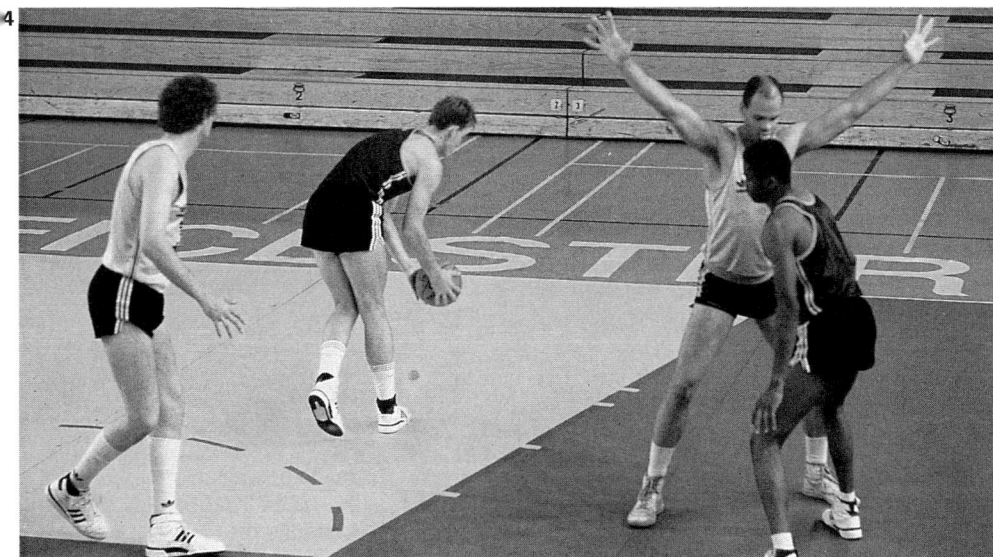

Three-on-three play

Three-on-three basketball can be a lot of fun because there are so many different options to employ both as an offensive and defensive exercise. Using three players allows for the three different positions of guard, forward-wing and a centre-power forward. Defensively this can help a team work on assignments such as screening, help-defence and handling mismatches. Offensively a team can work on specific options that are in their offence. Since most offences require the correct court balance a lot of offence comes from three-on-three plays.

Three-on-three pass and screen
O1 passes to O2 then sets a screen for O3

Three-on-three give and go
O3 uses screen to receive the ball. O1 rolls to the basket after screening

Three-on-three pass and screen

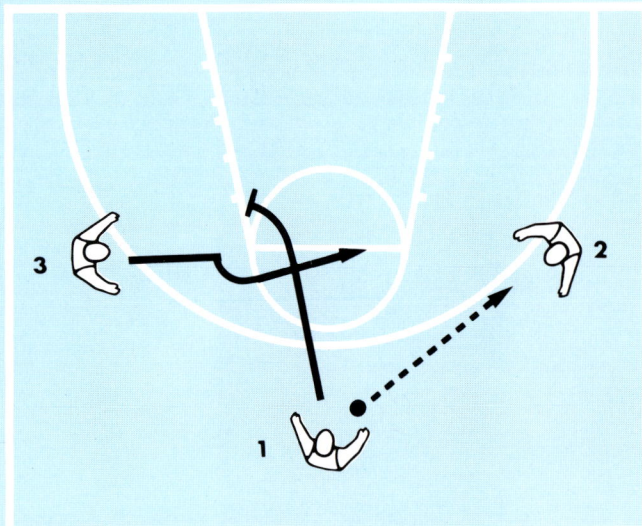

Three-on-three give and go

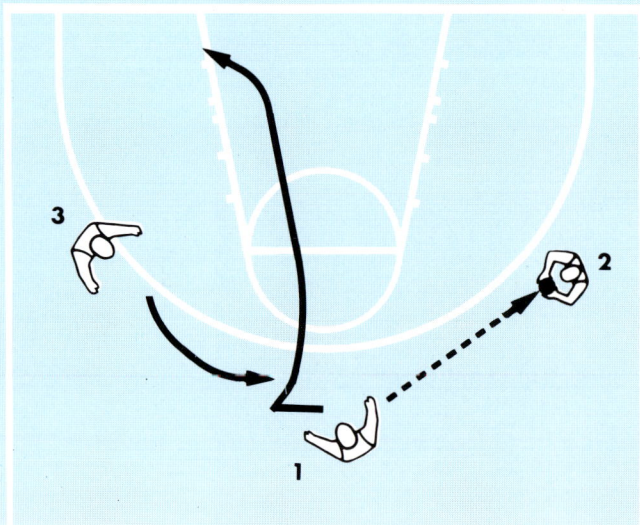

Pass and screen

This option can be used anywhere on court and is the basis of the motion offence. This idea of passing and screening keeps the offence moving and balanced with the bonus that it is tiresome for a defence to go through screens continually. It can also create mismatches between attackers and defenders forcing shorter players to guard taller players.

Offensive player O1 is the ball-handler and starts with the ball on the three-point line in the middle of the floor. O2 and O3 are on opposite wings to maintain floor balance. They work on getting open for a pass. O1 passes to O2 who will then sprint to the edge of the foul line and set a wide screen for O3. O3 must decide which way to use the screen, to fake going towards the top of the key and then cut to the basket or vice versa. After O1 screens he rolls to the basket and fills the unoccupied wing position. If O3 gets the ball at the top of the key he will pass and screen away. This sequence is continuous until a lay-up or an open jump shot is taken. Remember the offensive players must brush shoulders with the screener.

Give and go

This is the three-man version of the give and go. The drill starts the same as the pass and screen game. Offensive player O1, who is in the middle of the floor, passes to either O2 or O3 and then takes a jab step away from the pass and cuts hard to the basket and looks out back to the wing that he just passed to. The wing with the ball will try and pass to O1 if open, if not he will dribble to the centre of the floor, pass to the open team-mate and use a jab step and cut to the basket. This give and go is continuous with the players replacing each other until they have created the space for a good shot, preferably a lay-up.

Weave

Although not used as much as it was, this is still a good exercise for the three-on-three. Offensive player O1 starts in the middle and dribbles hard at O2 who goes around O1 for a hand-off pass, O2 continues with the dribble and hands off to O3. This weave is continuous with the players moving close to the basket aiming to drive or to shoot an open jump shot.

WHELTON'S TIPS

● *Three-on-three basketball helps players to learn to use each other and move without the ball. These fundamentals are the hallmark of good offensive basketball.*

Four-on-four play

Four-on-four games are mainly used to practise offence without using a post player. This can be a useful and effective practice for a team without a tall post player. The use of give and go plus pick and rolls are essential.

To begin playing four-on-four you should have two guards and two forwards. Players must keep the court balanced, which means they mustn't have two or more players in the same area unless they are setting a screen. Keeping the floor balanced will give the offence the opportunity to go back door, isolate a mismatch or isolate a weak defensive player. In a smaller team with no tall player the players should learn to play all the positions.

Pass-cut-replace

This four-on-four game places the guards spread wide a few feet deeper than the three-point line with the forwards starting in the corner areas. Guards will try and pass the ball to the forwards in a back door play if it develops. If not the guard will pass to forward 3 and cut to the basket coming out on the other side of the basket. Guard 1 will replace guard 2's position and forward 4 will move up to guard 1's initial position. The ball will continue to be passed and only when the ball is passed to the corners will there be a cutter. This game not only works on passing, back door plays and cutting but also makes the players react quickly to replacing their team-mates and thus getting used to the idea of keeping the floor balanced.

Pick and roll

With the players initially positioned the same way, work on pick and rolls with guard 1 and forward 3 and guard 2 and forward 4. This is excellent because it gives the players a side of the floor to execute the pick and roll. When two players are working the play make sure the two players on the weak side exchange positions to get used to moving without the ball.

Double picks

A double pick is two players setting the pick, side by side, to free a team mate. If you want to use tactics such as double picks you must make them part of your four-on-four play.

The players are positioned to balance the floor, guard 1 has the ball and passes to forward 3 who has freed himself on the wing. Guard 1 runs towards the opposite elbow (edge of foul line) where he is joined by guard 2. They both set a stationary double pick, side by side touching sneakers and both setting the screen. Forward 4 recognizes the play and jab steps towards the basket to get the defender leaning and then sprints up the lane using the double pick by brushing shoulders with the outside man. The

forward receives the pass and immediately tries to shoot. If this isn't possible he drives to the basket to score or passes to one of his team-mates in a scoring position.

WHELTON'S TIP

● *Replace, pick and roll and double picks are all part of offensive basketball that players should learn*

Four-on-four pass-cut-replace 1

1 Guard 2 passes to forward 3 then cuts to the basket with guard 1 replacing guard 2's position and forward 4 replacing guard 1's initial position

2 After replacing players are back to original alignment

Four-on-four pass-cut-replace 1

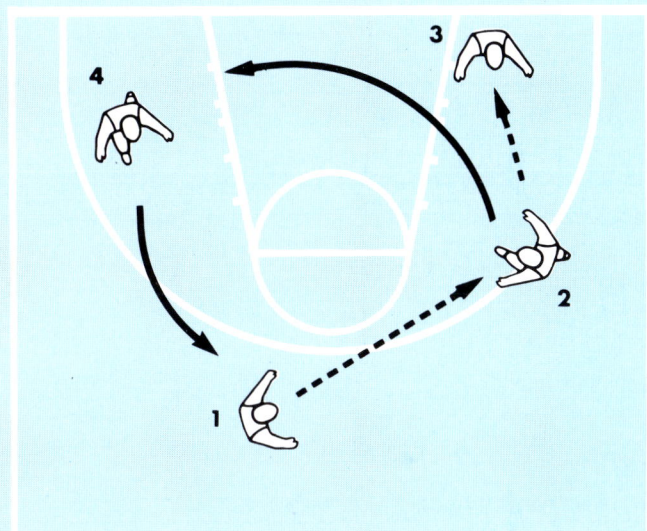

Four-on-four pass-cut-replace 2

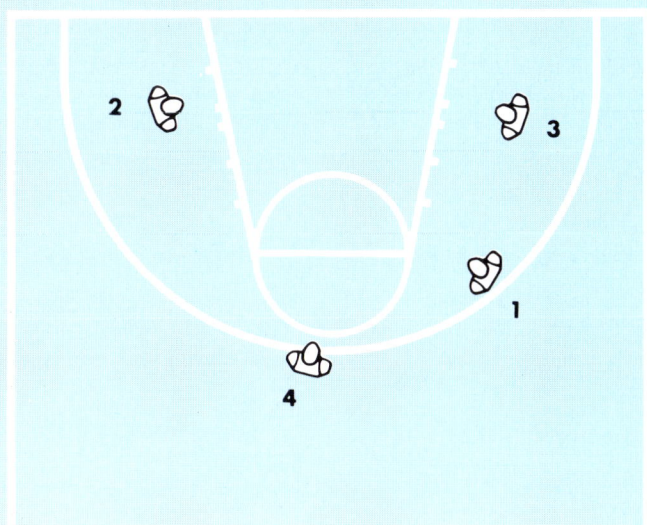

Five-on-five play

We've worked on two-on-two, three-on-three, four-on-four and now with the same tactics as give and go, pass and screen away we put in the final balancing piece, the player in the middle who we call the centre or pivot. The team is always striving for high percentage shots and the centre will help in that area because you will pass to him close to the basket. Everybody in the crowd loves the three-point shooter but players and coaches know that the guts of the team start at the centre position.

Start with four-on-four plays and put the centre in with the rule that he can't go out further than the foul line, working only from the high post down to the low post. Anytime the ball can be passed to the centre at the low post it must be done. This will give him the opportunity to go one-on-one against a defender or if the other defenders sag in on him he can pass the ball back out to the perimeter for a player to shoot.

When playing the give and go the centre is in the ideal position to be a receiver since his defender will probably help out on the player with the ball, leaving the centre open. If running pick and rolls the centre should position himself on the weakside to rebound. At all times the centre should pound the offensive boards. The centre becomes vital to the make-up of the offence. He is a scorer from the low post, a passer from the high post and a rebounder at all times.

Five-on-five action of the highest quality, with the Dallas Mavericks on offence against the Los Angeles Lakers in a match from the National Basketball Association

Final-minutes' play

Victory in close basketball matches depends on which team properly executes their offence in the final stretch. With the clock ticking away, the emotion of the moment can get the better of a team. That is where practice of last-minute situations can be vital to a team's season. A team must know, for example, which players should have the ball in the final moments of the game. Even some of the best players don't want the ball when the game is at a crucial stage. Here are some plays which my teams have used with some success when the score was close near the end of a game and we needed to score a basket.

Clear out

A clear out is when four members of the team make space for an offensive player to go one-on-one. When a team has an exceptional one-on-one player who can also handle the ball fairly well, just get out of his way! The player must be mature enough to handle the situation without getting carried away and forcing a bad shot. We have always told our players to at least get to the foul line by drawing a foul to earn a free throw. If you have an open shot take it, but if not try a series of fakes to draw a foul. (The clear out works best for guards and small forwards who can start 20 to 25 feet (6 to 8 m) away from the basket and create a shot. This is where the one-on-one moves will be used. You should receive the pass and immediately square to the basket in the triple threat position (page 78). A jab or rocker step will be useful.

High-low

This is an isolation play for a low post player.
  The diagram shows the 1-3-1 offensive alignment with the low post man having the freedom to move to get into position to receive a pass. If he is fronted by the defensive player try to lob past him. If he has the defensive player on his back try to get him the ball. The three perimeter players and the high post man pass the ball to each other to try and get the defensive player out of position. They only dribble when they have a clear lane to the basket. This is when the one-on-one post moves become very important as the player should at least go to the foul line for a free shot by drawing a foul from the defender.

Two-on-two isolation

With time running out and the ball in the hands of a guard it may work to run a pick or series of picks to get a jump shot from the guard or the tall player rolling to the basket after setting the pick.
  The diagram shows a play that allows the ball-handler the option of using a pick to his right or left. This may depend on which side of the floor he favours, which way the defensive player is facing him or who is setting the pick. In this

High-low

Two-on-two isolation

instance offensive player O1 decides to use O4 for the pick and roll. O2 recognizes this and clears the area. O3 has defensive responsibility while O5 moves in to rebound. After working on the pick and roll during practice, O1 and O4 should get a good shot or get fouled to win a free throw.

WHELTON'S TIPS

● *Practise last-minute situations so that you're ready for them in a game.*

● *Know which player in your team should have the ball for that final shot.*

High-low 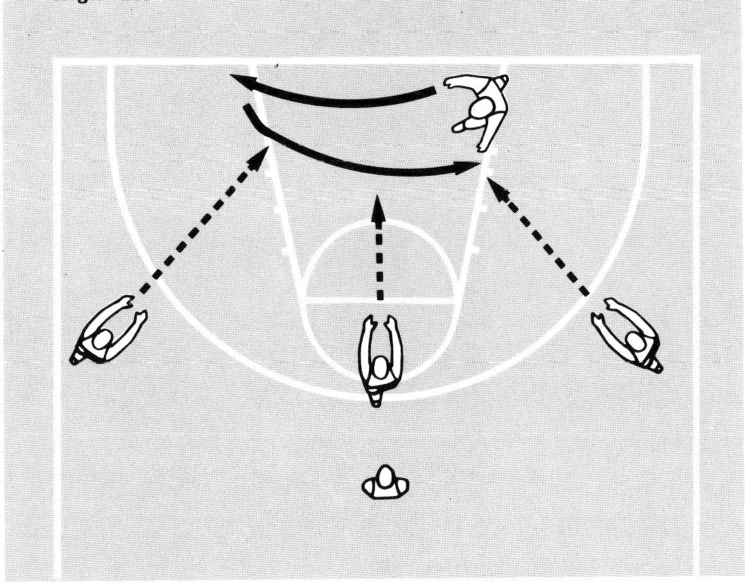
The three perimeter players and the player at the high post pass the ball between each other to try to draw the low post player's defender out of position

Two-on-two isolation 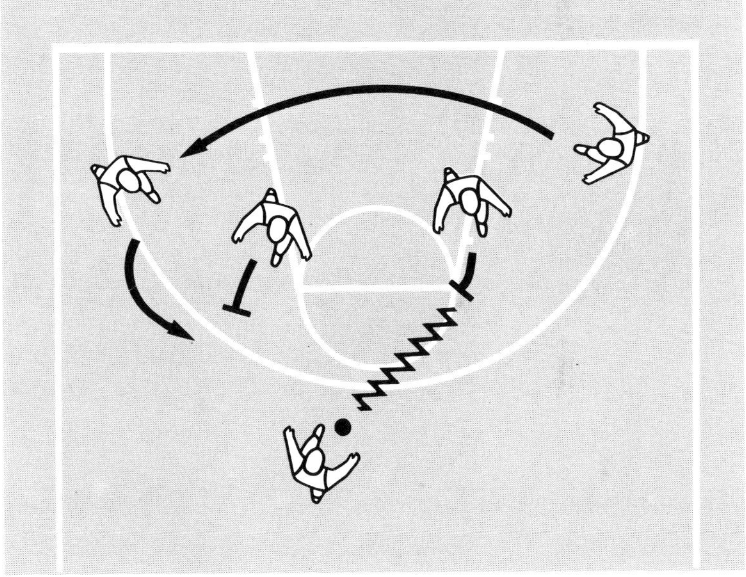
In the final seconds of the match you may need to get your ball-handler free to attempt a match-winning shot. You can use a pick to the right or left, while one wing moves to cover on defence and the other sees to rebounding

MAN-TO-MAN OFFENCE

' Man-to-man offence is used against man-to-man defence, and there are many different types of man-to-man offence. In some, players follow set patterns of play, while in others they are allowed to read the defence themselves and adjust accordingly. Some teams look a great deal better if they have as few rules as possible to follow – just tell them to go where the defence isn't! '

Bill Hanzlik in the strip of the Denver Nuggets

Opposite: Under intense pressure, the great Larry Bird of the Boston Celtics tries to make a pass across the defence of the Portland Trailblazers

Introduction

After deciding on your team's style of offensive basketball you must try and select players who fit into the system. If you want to play an up-tempo game you must look for players that are athletic and have quickness of movement as well as running speed. If you aim for control and want your team to concentrate on walking the ball up the floor and executing your half-court offence to a high percentage, you can afford to use taller and slower players and try to pound the ball close to the basket. This style of play will help the taller players stay out of foul trouble and they will not tire so quickly.

Man-to-man offences are used by teams to enable them to score versus the opponent's man-to-man defence. Offences should be used to benefit the talents of a team. Within the team concept a team will use tactics such as one-on-one, two-on-two, three-on-three, back doors and pick and rolls.

When selecting a man-to-man offence it is essential to evaluate the players first. There is nothing more frustrating for players than trying to execute an offence that doesn't suit them. The offence you select may be based on answers to such questions as: how many ball-handlers do we have; what is our inside scoring potential and from which players; what is our perimeter scoring potential and from which players; who can benefit from isolation plays (one-on-one); do we have the athletes to execute a motion offence?

If a coach asks his players to shoot accurately he cannot expect them to run out on court and do it. The coach has to help his players to create good shots through his selection of tactics.

There are different styles of man-to-man offence. Teams can run a patterned offence which allows set alignments and designated plays. There are also continuity offences which rely a lot on cutters, screeners and replacing (filling a spot created by a team-mate), and the motion offence which is put into the continuity category because of its uniqueness in allowing the players to read the defence and adjust accordingly.

With the NBA shot clock set at 24 seconds, the international clock at 30 seconds and the American college clock at 45 seconds, coaches have had to let the players play and I think that has been great for basketball. Too many coaches

Perimeter rules

● Don't dribble until after three passes have been made. The point guard initiates the offence by dribbling into a position to pass the ball. (Actually I always tell my players not to dribble at all, but we do feel that after three passes the dribble may be used to get the ball to the post player. If a player is using a worthless dribble, we certainly let him know!)

● Pass and cut to the basket if you don't receive the ball. Fill (replace) the nearest perimeter spot. Don't make the same cut twice running, but vary your cut from jump steps away from the basket, to an immediate cut to the basket or a pivot and roll to the basket.

● Pass and screen away for a perimeter player. Don't set the same screen twice running. Pass and immediately screen, pass, jab step to the basket and then screen; pass, replace an area, then try to screen. After every screen 'open up' or turn your body to be a possible receiver of a pass.

● Simply pass, go away and then return to your spot to be a receiver. This will help to keep the defender off balance and uncertain about your intentions.

● Don't stand for more than two seconds. Move without the ball, because if one player stands still it will create crowding of players which will disrupt the court balance.

● Unless an open player has a lay up, no perimeter player should attempt a jump shot until after five passes. Timing is so important in a motion offence and after this time the player will be in a good position to take a shot. The post player must have every chance to get the ball before you resort to shooting from outside.

● Pass to the high post when possible. The high post area is a good place to attack a defence. If the high post player is open try to get the ball to him. This will relieve the pressure on the perimeter players who can then look for their own scoring opportunities if the ball comes back.

Rules for post players

● Position one player at the high post and one at the low post. The only time this doesn't happen is when the players are exchanging positions or setting picks for each other. This will make it difficult for the defenders to help each other.

● Post players must work together. They aren't being selfish when they look for each other. When the high post player receives the ball he tries to pass down to the low post man who is trying to post up.

When the low post players gets the ball, the high post immediately cuts to the basket on the other side of the lane. This will result in a lay-up if the high post's defensive player cheats on the low post and leaves him free.

● Don't stand for more than three seconds. Allow three seconds for post players to give them the opportunity to post up.

● The high post player should try to set screens for the perimeter players. The low post, when

away from the ball, can set screens for perimeter players on the baseline. These picks can be very effective. The two post players are always looking for opportunities to set screens for each other in the post areas.

Team-mates can run all the various passing sequences, not only to practise the actual moves but also to develop their understanding as a team. You can run back door plays, pass and screen, give and go and divide the group to practise two-on-two moves. If your team are not making good L-cuts or V-cuts then run the moves with only cuts being allowed; if they're not setting good screens, then make these moves only allowing screens and picks, concentrating on passing and creating the openings for easy lay-ups.

Baseline screen 2

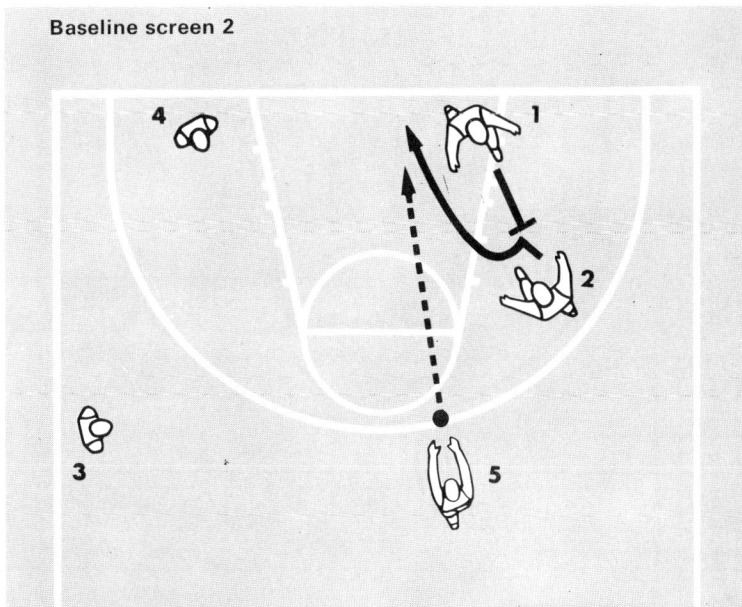

Baseline 3

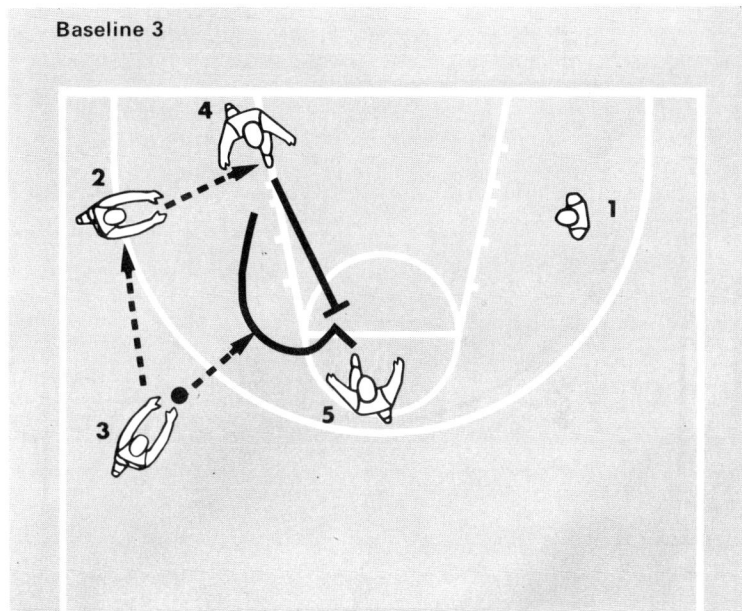

Baseline screen
1 O1 has set a screen for O3 and is using O4's low post screen for a lay-up

2 O2, realizing that O1 was not open, passes to the high post O5 and uses O1's screen for a lay-up

3 O2 was not open, so he clears to the corner. O5 passes to O3 and uses O4's pick and goes to the basket. O3 can pass to O5 or to O2, who may have a better angle to receive the pass than O5

Drills for motion offences

Keep away

Using a half-court area, there should be five offensive and five defensive players with the offensive players using the motion offence, remembering that nobody can dribble. A team gets one point for a completed pass, two points as well as retaining possession for scoring a lay-up. The first team to 50 points wins. The defence gets the ball by a turnover, a steal, a rebound or if the offence uses a dribble. This forces players to move without the ball while maintaining court balance.

Post drills

Using post players only, play two-on-two in the post areas only. Have two coaches passing the ball in from the wings, constantly telling the players to use each other on offence.

Perimeter drills

Play three-on-three basketball using the perimeter rules for motion offence (page 93). Put two post players in the high and low post area to set screens for the offensive players.

WHELTON'S TIPS

● *Use the high-post plays if you have a point guard who is a scorer*

● *The 1-4 is good if you have a point guard, wing players who are an offensive threat and two post players*

1-4 man-to-man offence

1 The point guard, O1, has the option of passing to any one of the other four players

2 O1 initiates the back door play by passing to O2. He could have passed to O3, and the back door play can be started by the move of either of the post players

3 O1 has passed to O5 who makes the back door pass to O3 as he makes his cut to the basket

4 The initial high-post option

5 Start by O3 passing to O5

6 Begin with O5 passing to player O2

7 Either wing player can use the double pick play

1-4 man-to-man offence 1

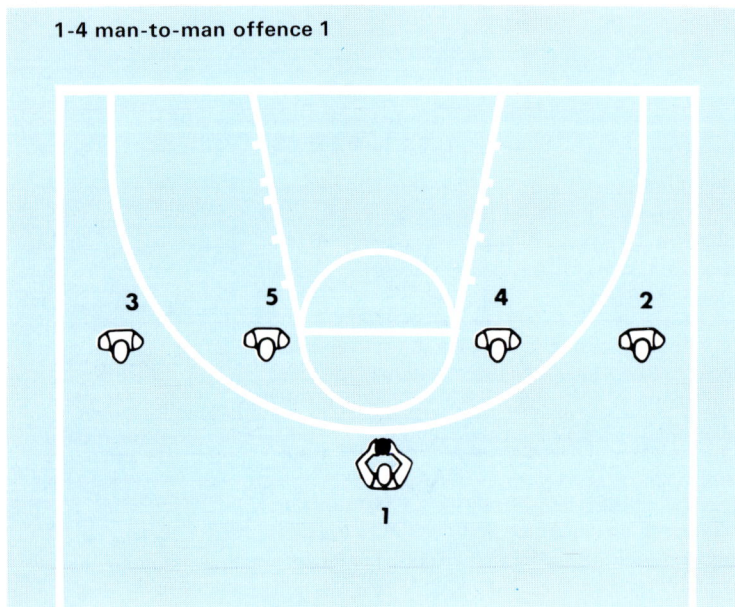

1-4 man-to-man offence

This offence is effective for a team that has a point guard, two wing players posing offensive threats and two post players. The 1-4 set gives you the option to run patterned plays, continuity plays and also to use 'automatics', or plays made spontaneously because of defensive movements. For example, a back door play (page 83) is an automatic.

The first diagram shows the initial alignment for the 1-4. Offensive player O1 is the point guard who has the option of passing to any of the four players. Having the floor spread leaves room for back door plays.

The second diagram shows the back door play from O1 to O2. Of course, O1 can pass to O3 if O2 is overplayed. The back door can also be run by passing to one of the post players first.

The third diagram shows O5 hitting O3 with a back door pass.

High-post plays

The 1-4 offence is useful especially if you have a point guard who is also a scorer. The 1-4 gives the player the opportunity to use high-post screens from two players.

The fourth diagram shows the initial high-post option. O1 passes to wing player O3, O5 sets a wide screen on the high post, where O1 tries to rub his players into the screen to get free for a lay-up.

The fifth diagram shows O3 passing to O5 who has stepped away from the basket to get free. O3 then sets a screen for O1 who pops out for a jump shot or goes back door for a lay-up. O4 sees that O5 has the ball and picks down for O2 who pops up the lane looking for his shot. The next option is made depending on where O5 makes his pass.

The sixth diagram shows what happens when O5 passes to O2. O5 immediately picks down for O3 who can go to the basket or use the screen and come up the lane looking for the ball. O2 can pass to O3 or pass to O4 who is posting up on the low post. A lob pass to O4 may be possible since O3 and O5 have cleared out the weakside help defenders by drawing them over to their side of the lane.

Double pick play

This play is effective for either wing player, especially if they can shoot from the perimeter. In the seventh diagram the picks are being set for O2. O3 and O5 set a double screen down low for O2 to rub his defensive player into. O2 must use these picks effectively by brushing shoulders with O3, who is the low player, and then cutting up the floor towards the O1. This will help leave the defensive player behind the screens. This play can also be run for O3 who will use the double screen set by O2 and O4.

1-4 man-to-man offence 2

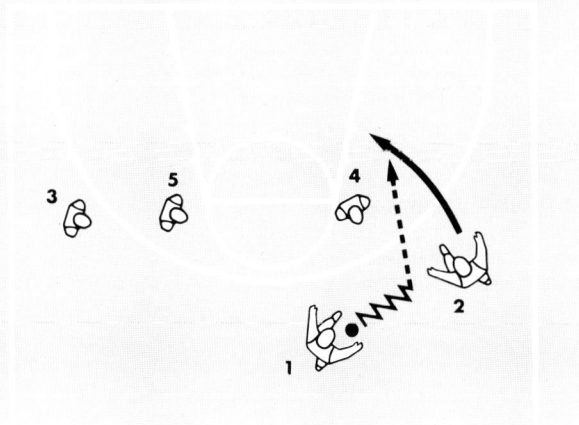

1-4 man-to-man offence 3

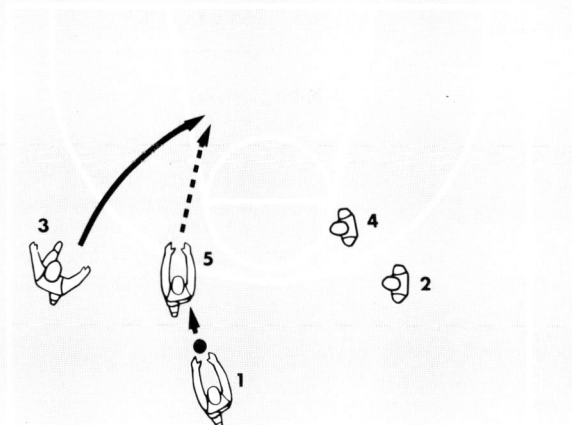

High-post option 1

1-4 man-to-man offence 4

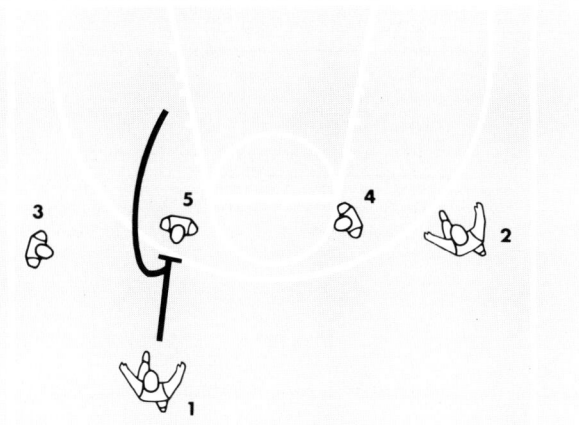

High-post option 2

1-4 man-to-man offence 5

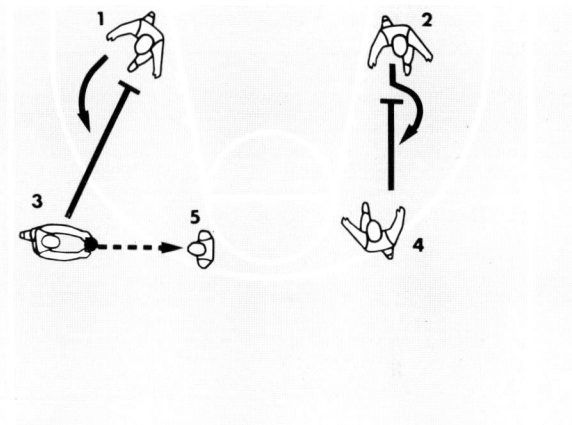

High-post option 3

1-4 man-to-man offence 6

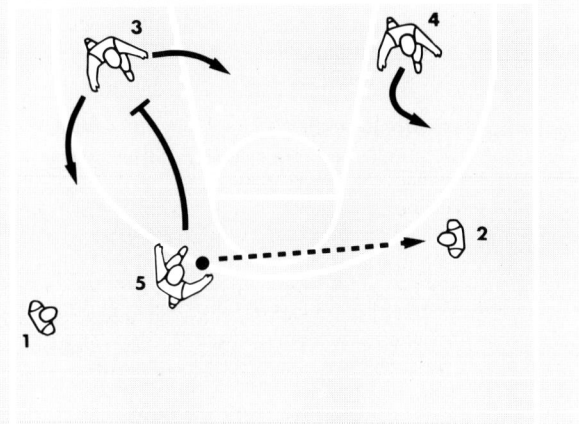

Double pick play

1-4 man-to-man offence 7

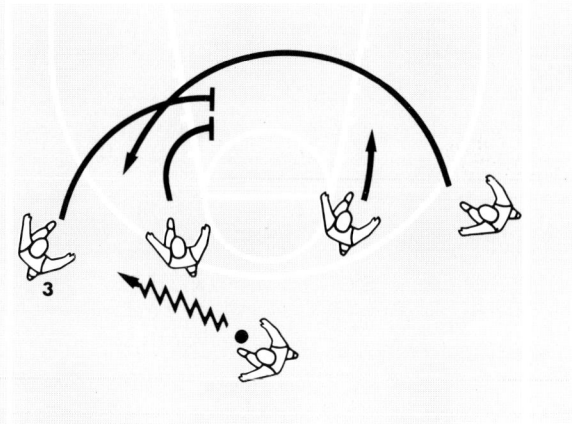

UCLA high post
offence
1 Initial alignment
O1 or O2 can have the
ball
2 Basic option
a The ball starts with O1
b O3 has passed to O5,
then screened down for
O1
c O4 has passed to O1
or O2 then screens down
for the opposite forward
3 Scissors play
O2 passes to O5 then
screens off for O1, who
scissors off for jump shot
4 Guard pick
Start out as the basic
option, with O1 using
O5's high post screen
5 Guard pick option
6 Double pick
To free a good jump
shooter, begin at the
basic option with O2
7 Double pick option
O4 and O5 set a double
pick to free O2

UCLA high post offence

The high post offence was made famous by University of California at Los Angeles (UCLA) which won an unprecedented and unrivalled ten American college championships between 1964 and 1975. The 1-4 and the high-post offence have similarities, but the high-post offence has a two-guard front and only one high-post player. This offence is most effective when a team has two guards who are both scorers, a high-post player who can pass well and shoot from the free-throw line and two forwards who are good inside players.

The first diagram shows the initial alignment of the high-post offence, remembering that either offensive players O1 or O2 may have the ball.

The second diagram shows the basic option with the ball starting with O1, who passes to player O3, then cuts off O5's screen looking for a lay-up.

The third diagram shows the next option with O3 having already passed to O5, then screening down for O1, who pops out looking for the jump shot. O5 can pass to O3 or O4, who is working for low-post position, or O2 who may have a better angle to pass to than O4.

The fourth diagram shows the basic option continued; O4 passes to O1 or O2. He will then pick down for the opposite forward.

Scissors play

This play is designed to free one of the guards for a quick jump shot or an inside shot from a screen.

The diagram shows offensive player O2 passing in to O5, then picking (setting a screen) for O1 who scissors off for a jump shot. If there is no shot, O1 can look for O3, who has used O4's screen.

Guard pick

This play starts out as the basic option with O1 using O5's high post screen. If O1 doesn't get a pass from O3 he goes across the lane and sets a screen for O4, as shown in the diagram.

After O5 sets O1's screen for O4 he screens down for O1 who comes up to the foul line looking for his shot.

Double pick

This is a play to free a good jump shooter for his shot. It can be run at any time during a game but may be saved for a last shot before half-time or the end of the game.

Start with O2, who begins with the basic option. O1 comes across to receive the pass from O4.

O5 and O4 both come down to set a double pick to free O2 for his shot, as shown in the diagrams.

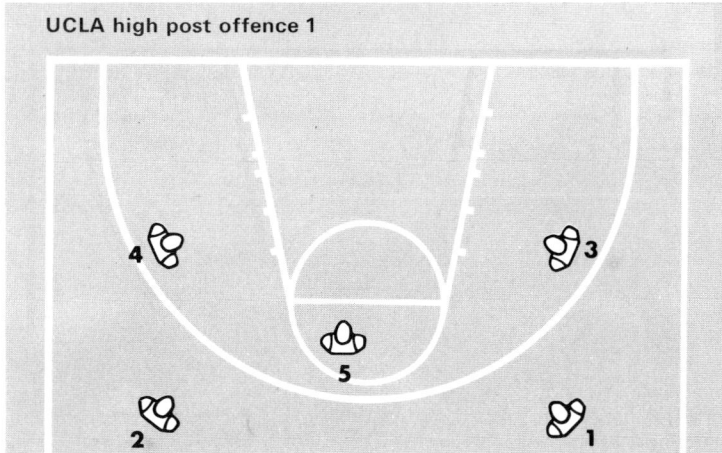

UCLA high post offence 1

Initial alignment

Basic option a

UCLA high post offence 2a

Basic option b

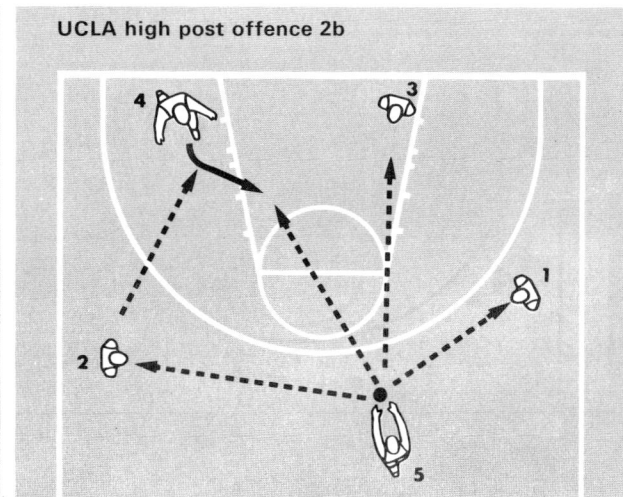

UCLA high post offence 2b

UCLA high post offence 2c

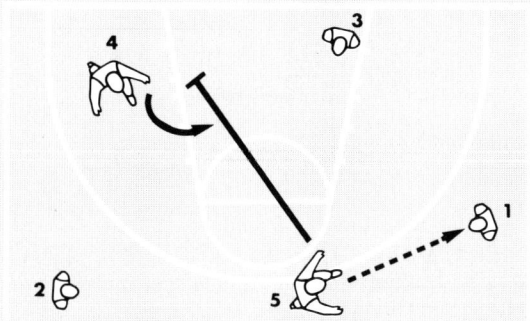

Basic option c

UCLA high post offence 3

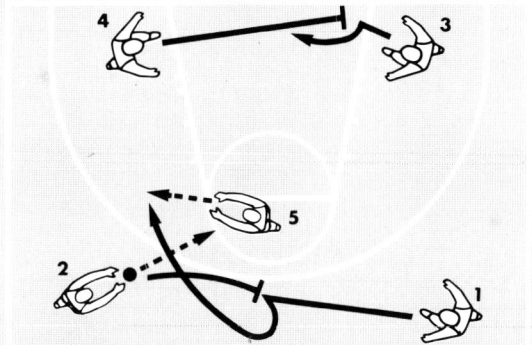

Scissors play

UCLA high post offence 4

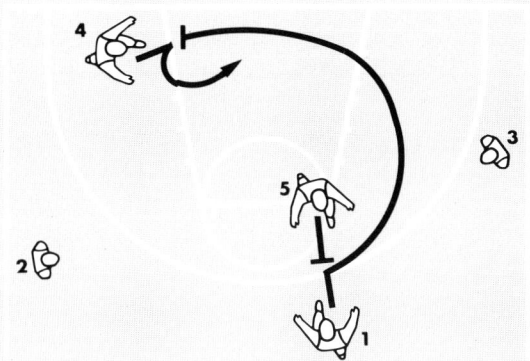

Guard pick

Double pick

UCLA high post offence 5

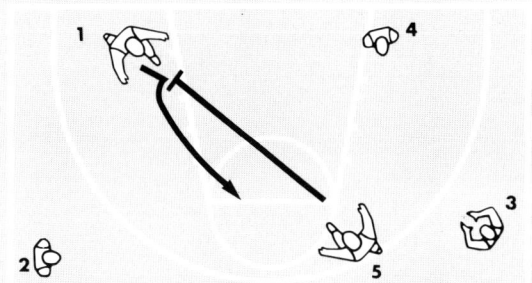

Guard pick option

Double pick option

UCLA high post offence 6

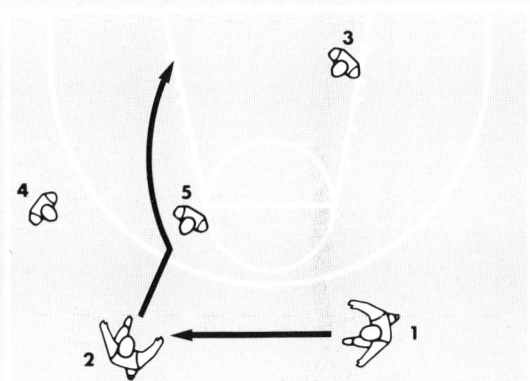

UCLA high post offence 7

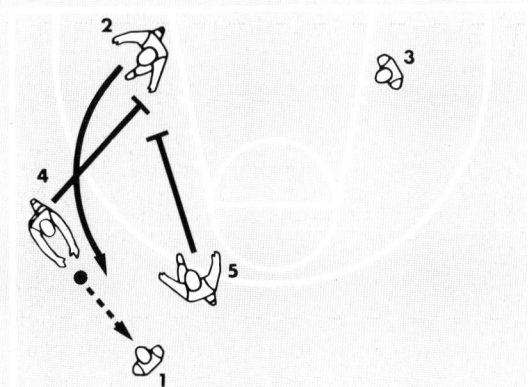

Fast break

This is quick movement of the ball down the court by a team which has gained possession. Teams may fast break off a turnover such as a steal or a bad pass; off a defensive rebound or off an opponent's successful field basket or a foul shot. Although not essential, foot speed and quickness are obvious advantages because the fast break can produce a basket in three seconds if a team reacts quickly.

Although a gamble and considered unsafe, the fast break has the potential effect of the quick knock-out punch. It should be a part of every team's game because it provides the opportunity to score a high percentage shot. Basketball is a game of 'streaks', or scoring phases, and the fast break can lay the opposition low with a series of quick attacks. Effective fast break teams can win basketball games in a five-minute stretch.

Before we go on to the specifics of the fast break here are some reasons for and against fast-breaking basketball.

For
● Fast break basketball puts pressure on the opposition and reduces them to making counter punches. Teams that fast break make things happen rather than just reacting to the opposition.
● Fast break basketball is fun for players and spectators. It seems to bring out the best in players.
● Opponents can't risk sending four or even three players to the offensive boards for rebounds since they will be worried about getting back on defence to cover your fast break. This obviously gives the fast-breaking team an edge in defensive rebounding.
● Fast breaking teams, especially when playing in front of a noisy home crowd, can prove to be intimidating to opponents.

Not only is it easy to create a lead in the game, but fast break basketball can also make it easier to catch up from behind.

Against
● Teams that run hard and fast trying to pass the ball to each other will obviously turn the ball over more often to the opposition. However if you work on having the ball in the right hands at the right time turnovers can be kept down to a minimum.
● Teams must be disciplined to know when a break is on and when not. They also have to know the score, how long there is to play

Fast Break
1 A defensive rebound has been taken and the fast break is under way with O4 passing the ball to O2, who is on his side of the floor

2 The fast break continues with the ball in the middle of the floor and O2 and O3 stay wide until they reach the foul line extended area

3 At the end of the fast break, O1 stays at the foul line to pass or shoot

Fast break 1

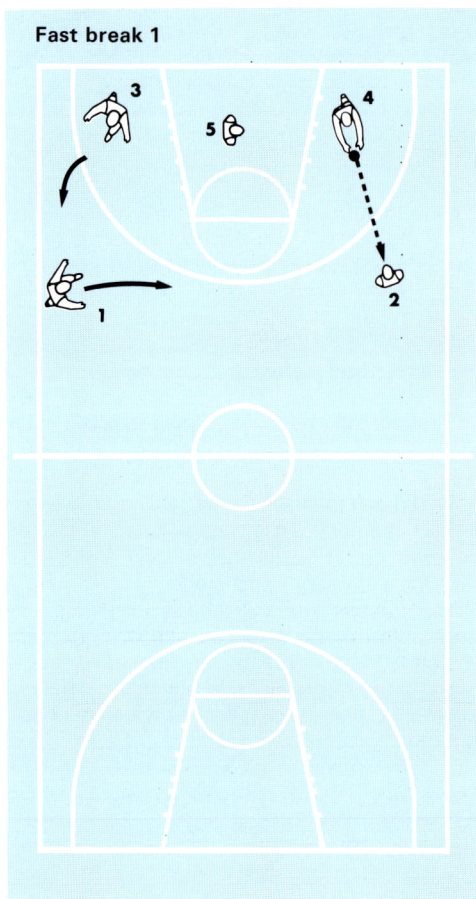

Fast break 2

ball he tries to make his open jump shot but if this isn't possible he dribbles towards the right corner.

O3 is a short forward who runs up the floor on the left side with the same rules as O2. He tries to make his jump shot after receiving the ball and if not, dribbles to the left corner.

O4 at first hesitates to make sure O5 doesn't need a second option on making the inbounds pass. When O1 gets the ball, O4 sprints up the middle of the floor looking for a long pass from O1. He must angle his body so that he can see O1 and be able to catch his pass without breaking stride.

The second diagram shows what happens if O1 pushes the ball up the floor with a pass to O2. O2 dribbles to the right corner if he doesn't have a clear drive to the basket or an open jump shot. O1 passes and now follows this pass until stopping at the foul line-extended area. O3 gives a quick look for a lob pass from O2, then stops and moves out to the left wing area. O4 always goes to the low post area nearest the ball. In this instance he is posting up on the right side, strongly trying to get the ball. O5 trails the play and always stops on the opposite of the extended foul line from O1.

The third diagram shows the players in a box formation with O2, O1, O5 and O3 spread out but still within shooting range while O4 is posting up. On transition from defence to offence it will be difficult for the defensive team to give help on O4 in the low post area. If O2 can't pass to O4 he immediately tries to swing the ball by passing to O1 who attempts a shot or passes to O4 who has now tried to move into position for a pass. O1 passes to O5 who has the same options as O3 if he receives a pass.

The fourth diagram shows O4 as the key man trying to get position for a pass. The same options would apply if the ball was passed up to O3 as to O1. O4 would post up on the left low post, O1 would follow his pass to the left foul line-extended area and O5 would stop at the right foul line area.

The fifth diagram shows what happens when O1 pushes the ball up with the dribble. O2 and O3 keep moving by crossing underneath the basket. This may help to free one of them by confusing the defence or rubbing off one of the

Secondary break 5

defenders against O2 or O3. To avoid collisions O2 crosses in front of the basket and O3 underneath.

The sixth diagram shows the same box formation with O2 now on the left wing and O3 on the right.

The seventh diagram shows the alignment for motion offence. O4 and O5 now pick for each other and O1, O2 and O3 use perimeter options of passing, screening away or give and go. As you can see the simple secondary break can bridge between the initial fast break and the half-court set offence.

5 As O1 tries to progress the ball with a dribble, O2 and O3 keep on the move by crossing under the basket

6 Box formation: Back to the box formation but with O2 on the left wing and O3 on the right

7 Into motion offence O4 and O5 pick for each other, while the other three use perimeter options of passing, screening away or give and go moves

Secondary break 6

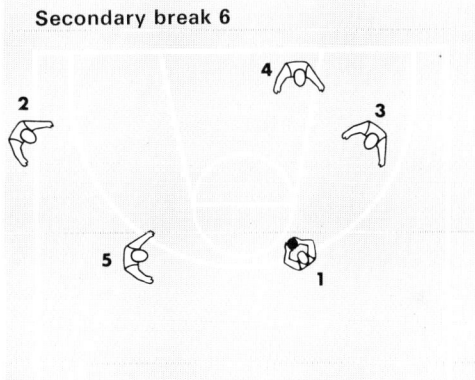

Secondary break 7

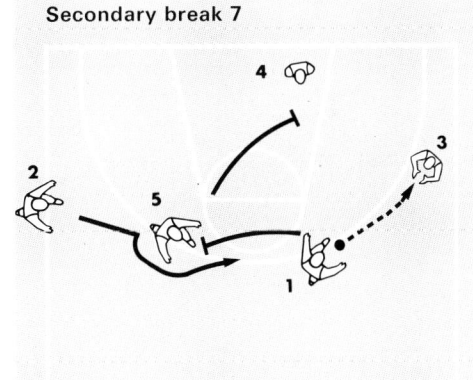

Zone offence

These are offences against zone defences and are usually different from man-to-man offence.

The starting point for thinking about a zone offence is to consider why teams play zone defence. Teams will play zone defence to stop inside scoring by forcing the offensive players to move outside to get a touch of the ball, to stop screening as part of the offence, to stop penetration and to force teams to shoot from the perimeter.

To operate a good zone offence you must use your players to try and do all these things: to move the ball inside, to use screens to set up shots, to penetrate by knowing where you can split the zone and to create opportunities for your best perimeter shooters.

'Splitting the seams' of a zone means moving offensive players into the gap between defensive players. This is done to force the defensive players to decide on area responsibilities, which may result in errors which benefit the offence.

The diagram shows the gaps in a two-three zone defence where offensive players could split the seams. Offensive player O1 wants to split the area between defensive players D1 and D2. This forces either D1 or D2 to stop O1's penetration. O2 and O3 will try and split the seams from the wing areas.

The defensive players have to stop O2 and O3's penetration or they will have a clear driving lane to the basket. These splitting movements will cause the defence to react and will weaken their coverage.

1-4 zone offence

The 1-4 zone offence alignment is best used against an even front zone defence, which is a defence with two defensive players at the top, such as the 2-1-2 or the 2-3. The 1-4 starts the offence away from the zone defence before moving to penetrate the zone.

The diagram shows the initial alignment of the 1-4 offence against a 2-3 zone defence. Offensive player O1 is the point guard who is always trying to penetrate whenever possible. His penetration will help create shots for his teammates. O2 is a wing player, either a guard or a forward who can shoot from the perimeter. O3 is the same as O2 but possibly a better rebounder. O4 and O5 are post players.

Options off the 1-4

The first diagram shows the movements of players when offensive player O1 passes to one of the wing players, in this case O2. The same movement would be made on the left side if the pass went to O3. O1 passes to O2 and takes one step towards O2 and one step in towards the basket. O4 slides down from the high post to the low post looking for the ball. If defensive player

Splitting the seams
The arrows point to the weak spots in a 2-3 zone

1-4 initial alignment
Initial alignment against a 2-3 zone

Options off the 1-4
These are the movements triggered by O1 passing to one of the wing players, in this case O2

Post cross
Quick ball movement around the perimeter, plus crossing by O5 and O4 should confuse the opposition about their defensive responsibilities

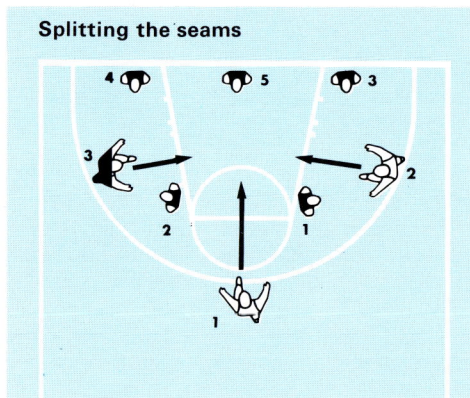
Splitting the seams

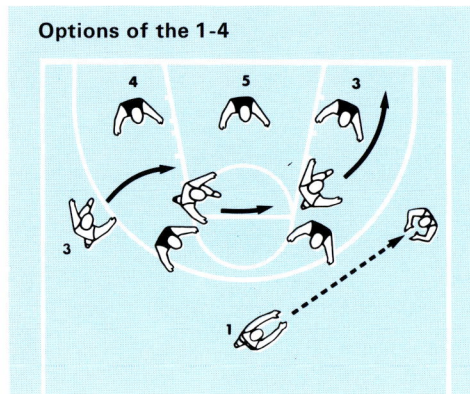
1-4 initial alignment

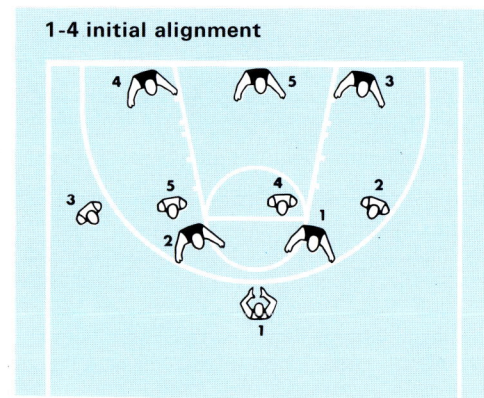
Options of the 1-4

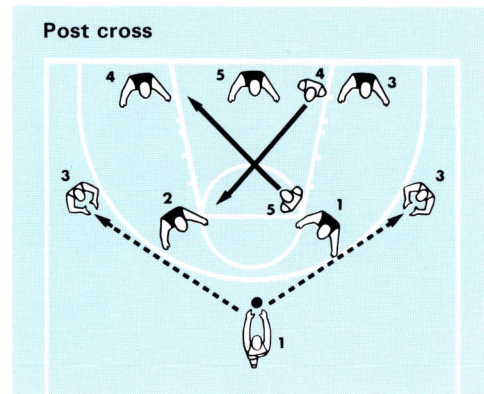
Post cross

D3 left his area to defend O2, O4 will be open immediately. O5 replaces O4 at the high post. If defensive player D1 leaves to guard O2, O5 may have an open shot from the foul line. O3 moves closer to the basket to become a rebounder.

In any zone offence, players shouldn't dribble unless forced to, nor hold on to the ball. The only way to force the defence to adjust is by quick ball movement. If O2 doesn't have a shot or a pass, try and move the defence by passing to O1 who will reverse the ball to O3. O3 may have a shot, but if not he will look for O4 or O5 who will cross as shown in the second diagram. The quick ball movement on the perimeter plus the crossing of the post players will confuse the defensive players about responsibilities.

1-4 overload
Overloading the zone is the tactic of overbalancing the floor by putting the majority of players onto one side of the zone. This will force zone defensive players to play against more than one player.

The first diagram shows overloading the right side of a zone out of a 1-4 alignment. O1 dribbles over, moving O2 to the corner. O4 moves to the low post. O5 moves to the high post. O3 moves to the rebounding position.

The second diagram shows the overload. The overload forces the defensive player D3 to play both O4 and O2 while defensive player D1 has to cover O1 and O5.

WHELTON'S TIPS

● *You must try to do everything a zone defence tries to stop you doing*

● *Get players inside to score from close range*

● *Penetrate because that is what the zone defence does not want*

● *Split the seams. Use crisp passes and quick movement to pull the zone apart at the seams and then move players into the gaps you create*

The third diagram shows a reversal of the ball to the left side and the movements to overload the left. O1 passes to O5 who has stepped out. O5 passes to O3 then goes to the low post area on the left side. O4 crosses O5 and moves to the left high post. O2 overloads the left by cutting underneath the basket to the left corner. O3 shoots or passes to O5, O4 or O2.

The fourth diagram shows the completion of the overload to the left.

> Force the defence apart by quick ball movement – don't dribble or hold onto the ball

1-4 overload
1 By overloading the offensive players on one side of the floor you force defenders in a zone to guard more than one player

2 The overload is forcing D3 to play against O2 and O4

Reversal
This shows the reversal of the ball and player movements which follow to overload the left side of the floor

Overload
The overload to the left has now been completed

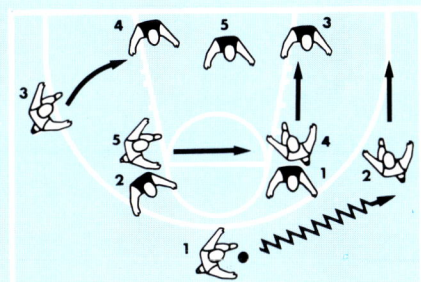
1-4 overload 1

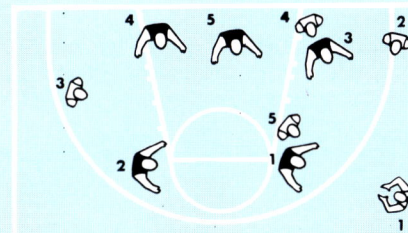
1-4 overload 2

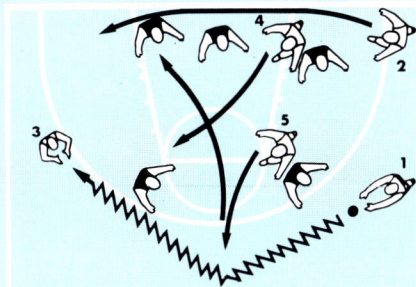
Reversal

Overload

WORK-OUTS

The skills of dribbling, passing and shooting the basketball are controlled by the hands and particularly the fingertips. For all these skills you need fingertip control. To make the ball do what you want, you must have strong, although not necessarily big, hands, strong enough to manage the hard and heavy ball.

Here is a programme for players to use during the season to sharpen their skills and in the off-season to improve their ball-handling. A problem I have seen with too many players is that they do not know how to practise. I can help you there, but to start this work-out all you need is the ball and a desire to improve your skills.

Warm-up

Injuries are a crucial element in stopping a player from making progress. Anytime you are going to exert yourself you must spend 10–15 minutes preparing your body for the work-out.

Mental preparation
Prepare yourself mentally to get the most out of your practice. Use this period to organize your time and to decide which aspects of your ball-handling you consider are the weakest, which therefore need the most work and what you can do to improve them. Motivate yourself to be the best and imagine dribbling the ball through opposing defences the way an Isaiah Thomas would do.

Strengthening
As part of your warm-up decide which parts of your body need the most strengthening to improve your control of the ball. Fingertip push-ups will help to strengthen the hands, fingers and arms. These are done like press-ups or push-ups but rather than balancing on the palms with the fingertips flat on the floor, put your weight on the tips of your extended five fingers. Don't be embarrassed if you complete only two or three. Sometimes the biggest and strongest players collapse after only a couple of fingertip push-ups, whereas the smallest guard may do 50 or more with ease. Even players with tiny hands can be seen palming a basketball with one hand because of the strength they've developed through hard work.

Squeezing a rubber baseball or squash ball will help strengthen the hands and wrists. Cup the ball with both hands using all ten fingertips.

Rotate the ball, while trying to squeeze the air out of it. When your forearms begin to ache, you know you're getting something from this exercise.

Ball-handling

Now we concentrate on improving a player's feel for the ball which will give him or her greater confidence in competitive play. Here are a series of drills to follow.

1 and 2
Finger push-ups

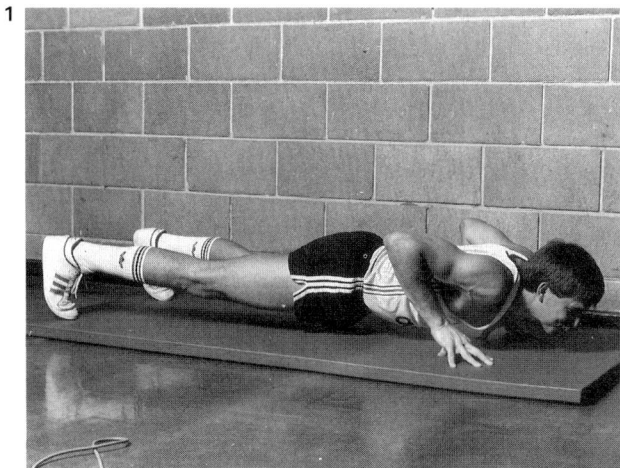

Squeeze

Using all ten fingers, squeeze the ball while rotating it in order to reinforce from the start that vital 'feel' for the ball, which must become second nature to you so that during play you can concentrate on how you are going to use your possession. (Drill time: 2 minutes)

Slams

Slap the ball from hand to hand, making it 'pop' each time you make contact. This is good for strength and developing a feel for the ball. Keep this drill going for at least 30 slaps.

Taps

Standing erect with your arms in front of you, tap the ball back and forth between your hands with the ball, just making contact with your fingertips. Your hands should be only a shoulder-width apart. Keep the ball moving as you move your arms over your head, then bring them down to your ankles and up again to the original position, using just the fingertips all the time. (Drill time: 1–2 minutes)

1 Stretching exercise for the legs

2 and 3 Ball taps

Step by step basketball skills

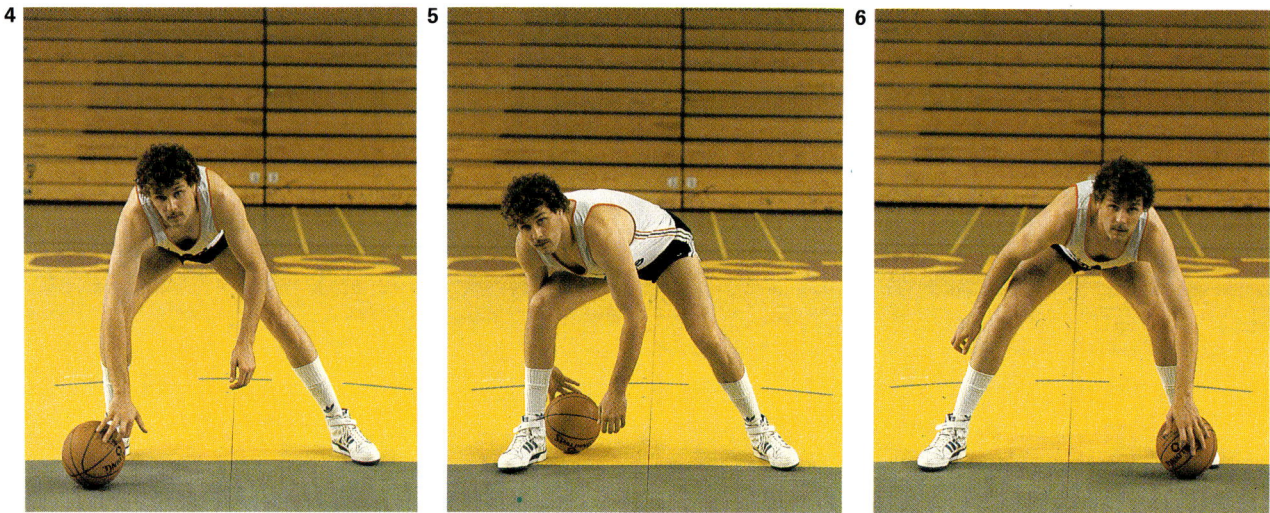

1-3 Round the world

4-6 Finger-tip figure-of-eight

7-9 Maravich drill

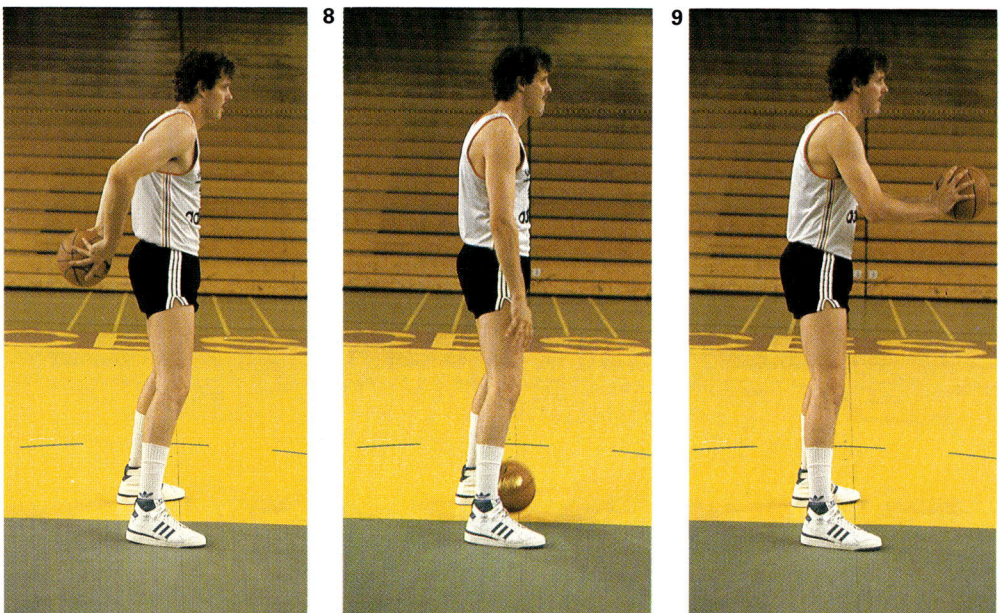

Round the world

Using both hands rotate the ball around your neck, your waist then your knees and ankles. Also put the ball through and around your legs in a figure-of-eight motion. Improve by rotating the ball as fast and smoothly as possible. If you drop the ball a few times to start with, don't worry, just pick it up and carry on.

(Drill time: 1–2 minutes)

Fingertip figure-of-eight

Place the ball on the floor with your legs spread wide. Using your fingertips only, put the ball through and around your legs in a figure-of-eight. Don't bounce the ball, just roll it as quickly as possible on the floor. Initially, roll it one way for at least ten figures-of-eight, then roll it the opposite way for at least ten more. It's important to keep your head up while doing this drill. Don't look down at the ball. You must develop a feel for where the ball is without looking at it.

(Drill time: 1–2 minutes)

Maravich drill

This was originated by one of the great showmen of college and professional basketball in the USA, Pete Maravich.

Spread your legs and hold the ball in both hands directly in front of you, waist high. Bounce the ball between your legs and catch it behind you at waist height with both hands.

Repeat the move, this time from the back to the front. This is excellent for developing speed in handling and for increasing the strength in your hands.

(Drill time: 1 minute)

Dribbling

Now that you have warmed up and worked on your ball-handling drills to develop that all-important feel for the ball, it is time to work on dribbling and applying those skills to game conditions.

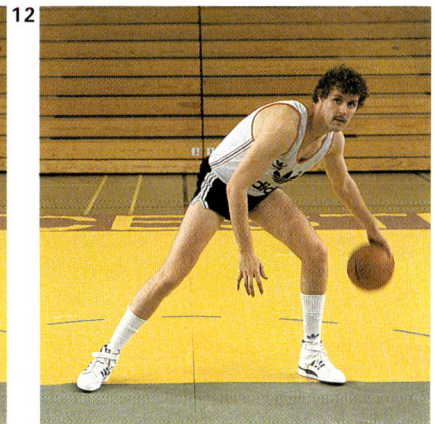

Dribble figure-of-eight

Spread your legs as for the fingertip figure-of-eight, but dribble the ball through and around your legs, changing hands in the middle. The dribble should be as close to the floor as possible. Complete 25 figures-of-eight one way, and then do 25 more in the opposite direction. It's important to use your fingertips and bounce the ball as often as possible in each figure-of-eight. Keep your head and eyes up, looking straight ahead. (Drill time: 1–2 minutes)

High-low

Starting with either hand bounce the ball as high as you can while standing still. After 10 to 15 high bounces bring the ball as close to the floor as possible while still bouncing. Squat or get down on one knee to keep the ball low. Repeat, alternating to the opposite hand. (Drill time: 1 minute)

Weak hand dribble

Using your weak hand, dribble up and down the floor at half to quarter speed, keeping your head up at all times. Dribble high, dribble low and change speed to help develop your weak hand. (Drill time: 2–3 minutes)

Through the legs

Walk up and down the floor dribbling the ball between your legs with every step. Once you're confident doing this, step up the challenge by continuing the dribble as you return down the floor backwards still bouncing the ball between your legs with every step. (Drill time: 2–3 minutes)

Game conditions

The only way to improve is to work as hard in practice as you do during a game. Use all the different dribbles covered in the book: the controlled, the speed, the crossover, the spin, the between-the-legs and the behind-the-back. Spend an equal time on all these dribbles, imagining defenders standing in your way to help you react. Refer now to the material on dribbling (page 10).

10-12 Dribble figure-of-eight

'Legs are the most important part of your body when shooting the ball, because all the strength to shoot comes from the legs '

Passing

Practising passing the basketball is often neglected or not taken seriously by many players, but passing is a skill that must be worked on just as much as shooting and dribbling. Players seem to take for granted the techniques involved in making the different passes, but it is obvious that the more you practise the more accurate and the crisper your passes will be.

Warm-up
Passing the ball to a team-mate or against a wall is a good way of warming up, apart from the benefit it will have on the skill.

Practice
A player practising alone should stand 4 to 5 ft (1–1.5 m) away from a wall and practise the different passes, keeping them going in rapid fire to improve speed, strength and reactions. Then sharpen peripheral vision by making a mark on the wall, and trying to hit it with the ball while looking slightly away.

When there are two players for the practice session they should stand 15 ft (4.5 m) apart and use two balls, making simultaneous passes by using all the different techniques.

When there is a large group of players, play two-on-two, three-on-three, four-on-four and five-on-five with no dribbling allowed. This will force the players to concentrate on the accuracy of their passes.

Shooting

Shooting can be improved only by practice. But that doesn't mean wandering out onto the floor and just aimlessly shooting the ball round. You must organize your time beforehand and go into the practice knowing what you're going to do: practise shooting off a dribble, without a dribble, going right, going left, starting with your back to the basket, shooting lay-ups, hook shots.

Here is a programme that will improve your shooting.

Warm-up
It is always best to practise shooting when you're tired. Run through some of the ball-handling work-out before moving onto shooting to simulate game tiredness, which will in turn affect your shooting.

Mental preparation
Before beginning the practice, collect your thoughts on how to make 'that perfect shot' and remember the checkpoints – fingertips, elbow in, flick the wrist, follow through.

Strengthening
Legs are the most important part of your body when shooting the ball, because all the strength to shoot the ball comes from the legs. Skipping, distance running and lifting weights are ways to build up strength in your legs.

1 Look for exercises that help warm up as well as develop a particular skill. Passing the ball against a wall, if you don't have a partner, is a good example of a doubly useful drill

2 Stretching exercises are another important part of warming-up, helping you stretch muscles before sudden exertion in a match. Muscles which are cold and tight are more likely to suffer strains and other injuries. Always loosen your muscles before playing

1

2

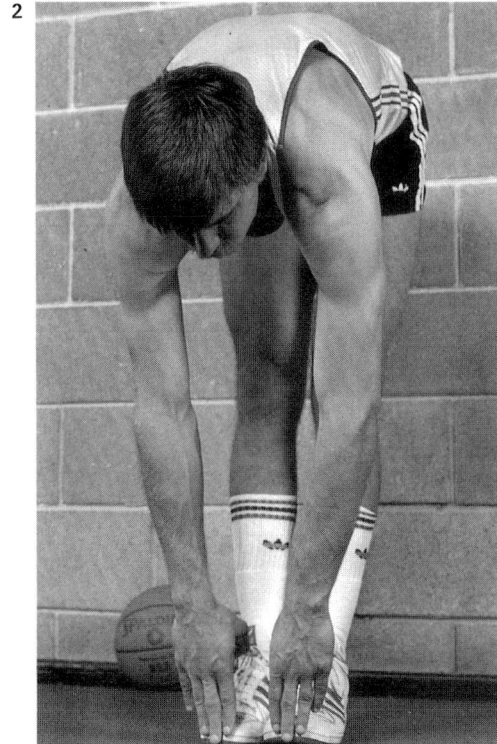

Technique

You must have mastered the mechanics of the shot before you can hope to develop your skill into becoming an accurate shooter, and this can be accomplished by repetition.

Step-by-step

Stand squarely in front of the basket and if right-handed put the ball in your right hand and bend your knees, extend your arm, flick your wrist, let the ball roll off your fingertips and follow through by waving goodbye to the ball as it leaves your hand. Take ten one-handed shots and aim to swish the ball cleanly through the net every time.

Take one step back and now use your left hand as the guide. Try for a clean swish and when this happens, take one step further back and repeat your shot. When you reach one step beyond the foul line make sure that every shot is a jump shot, concentrating on maintaining your technique by producing the strength for the shot from your legs.

Go as far back from the hoop as you can while still comfortably swishing the ball through the net. Once you have started to struggle to score you've reached the limit of your shooting range.

Skipping is another excellent exercise, encouraging nimbleness of foot, co-ordination, stamina as well as strengthening and loosening muscles

Shooting
Without a dribble

After working on reinforcing your technique, move to a different area of the court, catch the ball, square up and shoot. Keep your legs moving after the shot, because in a game you'll have to be constantly moving to get open for a shot. If there is no-one to pass the ball to you, just spin the ball back to you off one bounce, simulating a pass.

With a dribble

This drill is identical to the last one, but when you receive the ball use one hard dribble in either direction, square up and shoot. Ensure that you make a definite move with the dribble, because in a game you will have to beat a defender to find space to make your shot.

The grip on the ball for a right-handed shooter, showing the left hand acting as the guide and support until the moment the shot is released by the right hand

Rebounding

Warm-up
Make sure you stretch well, since your body will be extended to the limits during the rebounding work-out.

Mental preparation
There are no shortcuts, just the long route to success. Get yourself prepared to sweat, be banged around, grabbed and held.

Strengthening
Being strong is a must for a rebounder. Since rebounding is a very tiring job there has to be great attention paid to improving endurance. Weight training (page 112) will help to strengthen the legs, shoulders and arms to withstand the contact on the floor. Skipping, running up stairs and distance running all help strength and endurance.

Rebounding
Board taps
Start out by standing in front of the backboard and jump up and down touching the board each time with both hands. Keep your arms up and outstretched, touching the board ten times. Work on increasing your count to 50 or 60.

Tip-ins
This is an excellent offensive rebounding drill. Start in a semi-crouch on the right side of the basket. Throw the ball up off the backboard, concentrating on timing by tipping the ball at the peak of your jump. With your right arm and fingers outstretched, control the ball by tipping it off the board with the fingertips. Tip the ball with a flick of the wrist as if you're shooting. Tip the ball ten times against the board and on the eleventh, tip it into the basket. Now try the drill from the left with the left hand.

Ball high drill
Stand to the right of the basket, halfway between the backboard and the foul line. Start in a semi-crouch and throw the ball up high off the backboard. Catch the ball on the rebound at the peak of your jump, come down on your toes, but keep the ball in both hands raised overhead and shoot. The key is not to bring the ball down below head height.

In between each drill, while tired and blowing for breath, shoot some foul shots.

Ball high drill
1 Throw the ball up high off the backboard.

2 Catch the ball at the peak of your jump, coming down on your toes but keeping the ball held aloft over your head

1 and 2 If you don't have a backboard in a gym to practise board taps, you can always use a wall. Keep your arm stretched above your head and repeatedly jump to touch a line between the bricks, gradually building up to jump 50 or 60 times

3 Put the ball up against the backboard

4 After catching the ball, try a shot at the basket. The object is never to let the ball come down below head height

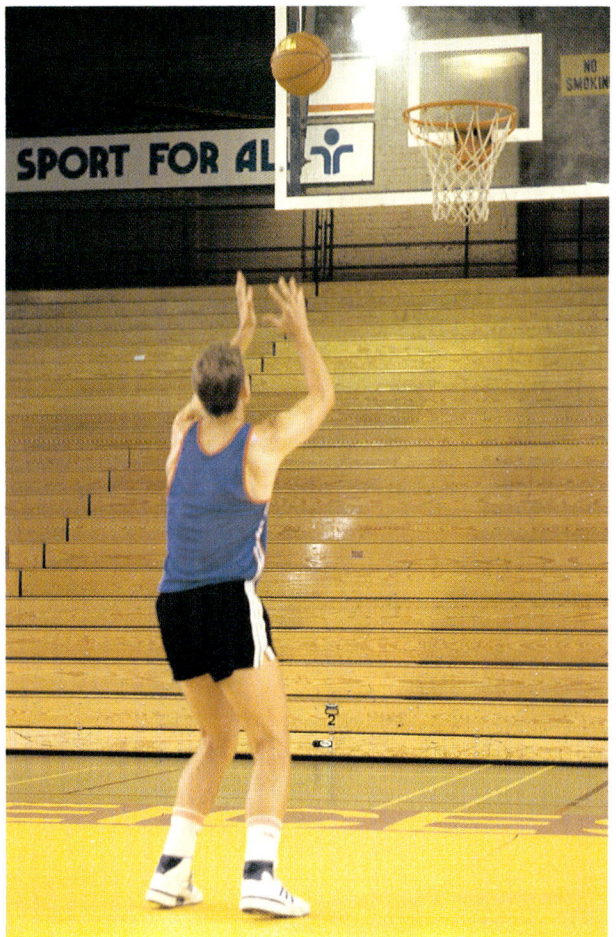

TRAINING AND PRACTICE

Training and diet

Basketball is a sport that requires physical skills such as shooting, rebounding, passing, jumping and running. Playing matches and taking part in training sessions demands mental alertness as well as physical readiness. A basketball player must work on both the physical and mental aspects of the game all year round. You must be committed to improvement because there are no short cuts. It's so important that you take the time to try and understand your body and how you can improve it.

Diet
Although all of us like to enjoy foods that are not essential, it is vital to understand those foods that are. If you eat the foods that are necessary to maintain peak performance, occasional sweets, candies or snack food will not cause a problem.

There are four food groups that players must select from to enable their bodies to function properly.
● Dairy products (such as milk, cheese, yoghurt, ice cream and eggs)
● Cereal foods (such as rice, pasta, bread and cereals)
● Meat, poultry and fish
● Fruits and vegetables
Players must select a variety of foods from all

these groups to ensure a balanced diet. If you eat the right foods you will not need supplements. Although there is nothing to suggest that players who take supplements, such as vitamins, are harmed by them, they should not be used to cover up poor eating habits. A pre-game meal should be eaten four hours before the match and should include foods from the four basic groups.

Conditioning
Basketball is a running and power game. To be ready to perform, you must not only strengthen your muscles, but also condition the heart and vascular system.

Cardiovascular conditioning will improve the flow of oxygen to the muscles, enabling you to perform without using up so much energy and so improving endurance. Aerobic training is part of this cardiovascular training and involves running for 3 to 4 miles (5 to 6.5 km) or more than 20 minutes. This running should be the starting point for off-season conditioning programmes.

Interspersed with the aerobic training is anaerobic training, which is particularly relevant to basketball players. Anaerobic training involves short, sharp bursts of activity such as sprinting.

Weight training
Weight training has become an important component of a basketball player's training programme. Until the 1970s weight training was thought to be unsuitable for basketball players

1 A weight machine is being used to strengthen the legs

2 The machine is being used to strengthen the arms, a very important part of the body for a basketball player

hy making their muscles too tight restricting their ability to stretch and jump. This became a myth as better understanding of weight training developed.

Bench press
Lie on your back on a flat bench with your feet on the floor. Grip the weight bar in both hands and bring it down to the chest before pushing it fully up until the arms are extended.

Curls
Sitting on a flat bench grip a dumbell in each hand by your side, alternately lifting each bar up to your shoulder then slowly letting it drop down.

Squats
Spread your feet as wide as your shoulders, holding the weight bar behind your head and about 2 in (5 cm) below the shoulder. Keeping the bar in that position and your back straight, squat slowly down and then back again.

Dumbell row
Stand with one leg slightly in front of the other and with the back bent, lifting the dumbell up to the shoulder and lowering it to the floor.

Toe raises
With the weight bar held as for the squat exercise, stand upright and lift onto your toes, holding that position for five seconds, before coming down then repeating.

Be a winner
Just as important as physical conditioning is mental conditioning. 'Mental toughness' are two words often used in the world of sports. Make no mistake, this toughness has to be practised and developed just as much as physical strengthening. Concentration is the key to winning basketball matches, especially when playing away from home.

When I am looking at a player as a possible recruit for my team I like the chance to study him playing in close matches when he is having a hard time. Those are the nights when you can tell if a player is a winner. I was once looking for a small forward for our team and I had the opportunity to watch three contenders for that position play in different matches at the same tournament. At first two of the players looked to be head and shoulders above the third. But after the days had gone by and I had watched all three very closely I turned to a coaching friend and asked: 'Why do I feel better about the player with less talent?' His reply was 'Because he shows the biggest desire to win' and it rang through my head like church bells.

Winners will make sacrifices, work hard and believe in themselves – qualities which are contagious and will benefit their team-mates. Great players are only truly great when they can make their team-mates into better players.

Kit and equipment

Most players are introduced to basketball either at school or by attending a club. The school or club will have the use of a court and basketball and rings, but if players are to develop their skills they will need their own basketballs and rings.

Ball
The basketball should be of good 'practice' quality that can withstand the rough handling that a drive or concrete surface will exact on it. Moulded rubber or nylon wound balls can be bought at a reasonable price.

Ring
Rings need to be fixed away from any windows and at a height of 10 ft (3 m) from the floor or ground. They can be placed at the side of a house, above a garage or to a post. They must be fixed to a hard area of board so that the player can shoot the ball off the board and into the net. Patios or drives make an ideal surface under the ring, but on no account site the ring over grass.

Footwear
The most important item of a player's personal equipment is footwear. The amount of running, jumping, twisting and turning involved in playing the game means that the player simply must have dependable and comfortable footwear. The footwear must give support to the ankles, have a firm grip on the floor and a thick sole to cushion the effects of continual jumping and landing. Players wear either shoes or boots, but most of the taller players tend to wear 'high-cut' boots as they feel they give more support to the ankles.

There are many specialist basketball boots and shoes on the market now and players can try different styes and makes until they settle on one that suits them. A player with weak ankles can buy ankle supports, although some of the specialist boots do have ankle supports.

Many players wear two or three pairs of thick soft socks to cushion the effect of jumping and landing. A good tip to remember when wearing a new pair of boots is to put a lot of talcum powder inside the inner pair of socks, to help prevent blisters caused by the friction of feet and boots.

Clothing
The remaining components of the basic playing kit are vests and shorts. These should allow the freedom of movement to play the game unrestricted. A track suit is essential as players spend up to half game time on the bench waiting to be substituted into play, and they must keep warm. The track suit should be easy to remove, so the player can get ready quickly to go on court. Finally, the player will need a sports bag.

Mike Burton
Manchester United coaching staff

'Winners will make sacrifices, work hard and believe in themselves'

If a player 'plays tired' he is more likely to get injured than if he is rested before a game

In-season discipline

In-season training doesn't start and end with the training session. There is much more to the season than what happens on the court during practice and matches and you must start by being healthy. At least two or three weeks before the start of pre-season training every player should have a full physical examination by their family doctor or the team doctor. There should also be a team talk concerning diet and nutrition. It should be clearly outlined to players what to eat and what to leave alone. There should be individual attention given to those players who have been asked to either lose or gain weight.

Rest

The question of rest and recovery must also be considered. Since a season consists of four of five months for school players, six to seven months for college players and up to ten months for players in national leagues who also play international basketball, rest is of the utmost importance.

If a player 'plays tired' he is more likely to be injured than if he is rested before a game. It takes a player up to 48 hours to recover fully from a hard work-out. 'Rest' doesn't mean doing nothing at all. During recovery days players should do stretching exercises or take long walks – but keep it gentle and leisurely. Players should balance their physical exertion by staying mentally alert.

Toe raises against the pressure of weights on the shoulders

Reading, studying and other mental activities are a fine counterbalance to playing and training.

Although sleeping habits obviously vary, players should try to have a good eight hours per night. Of course there are stories of players staying out most of the night, then still performing well on court the next day. But my experience has been that this type of behaviour always catches up with the player sooner or later.

Drugs

We can't ignore the question of drugs, after all the publicity there has been in recent years over drugs and the athlete. Drugs have brought players life bans, prison sentences and even, in the case of top American college star Len Bias, death.

There can no longer be any doubt about the effects of drug abuse. There are times when the biggest challenges to an athlete come off the court, and he must be ready to face them as well. A player owes it to himself, his family, his supporters and his team to learn to say no.

Flexibility

Athletes should always be looking for ways to better themselves. The use of stretching exercises to improve flexibility can definitely improve performance. Dancers and gymnasts stretch as part of their training because they have long realized the relationship between flexibility and performance. Limited flexibility results in restricted movement which can ultimately lead to a player spending a lot of time out of action due to muscle pulls, strains and tears. So, not only will flexible players be less tired, they will also be less prone to injury.

Close-season training

I believe that basketball players are made during the off-season. An advantage of basketball is that players can isolate individual skills and work on them without any other player taking part. The endless hours of practice spent in empty gyms, gardens, parks or even just dribbling the ball up the drive can produce great self-satisfaction. The players who want to become the very best use this time to improve their skills, and after a long summer they return to their teams as better players.

But what else can a player work on apart from actually playing? A total conditioning programme that includes speed, strength, muscle and endurance and flexibility will help. But remember, conditioning is more than just running, it is every activity that helps the player reach for new goals of performance. Here are some helpful hints to aid conditioning during the close season.

Strength training

- Always warm up first and use stretching exercises for the arms and legs
- Concentrate on carefully using the correct techniques when lifting weights
- Take a few moments before lifting to prepare yourself mentally. Think about what you're going to do and concentrate on the task. This will develop the intensity to help you lift better
- Always try to have someone to work with. Even though you can practise on your own, a partner will help with motivation and you can push each other to higher levels of performance
- Work on the most important muscles first: those in the arms, legs, chests and shoulders
- Use dumbells and bars to work muscles at different angles
- Vary your weight training by working heavily one day on certain muscles, then moderately in the next session
- To develop strength and muscle size use the overload principle. There are three ways to overload muscles. *Intensity*: Take only brief rests between sets of exercises. *Resistance*: Increase the weight you lift. *Repetitions*: Increase the number of times you lift the weight in each set.

Running

Before running, a player should spend between 15 and 20 minutes on flexibility exercises. A torn muscle will set a player back many weeks in his close season programme of training, so don't risk it! As for running, remember you are a basketball player, not a track star, so you don't have to impress anyone with setting new track records. Since we are talking about the close season, here is a plan to be followed over a ten-week spell. These runs should be undertaken on three days each week, preferably on days when you're not taking other exercise or training.

Training schedule

Week 1
Day 1: jog 1 mile (1.5 km), relax, jog $\frac{1}{4}$ mile (400 m)
Day 2: jog 1$\frac{1}{2}$ miles (2.5 km), relax, jog $\frac{1}{4}$ mile (400 m)
Day 3: jog 1 mile (1.5 km), run 1 mile, relax, jog $\frac{1}{4}$ mile (400 m)

Week 2
Day 1: jog 2 miles (3 km), relax, jog $\frac{1}{4}$ mile (400 m)
Day 2: run 1$\frac{1}{2}$ miles (2.5 km), sprint 220 yd (200 m), relax, jog $\frac{1}{4}$ mile (400 m)
Day 3: run 1 mile (1.5 km), jog 1 mile (1.5 km), relax, jog $\frac{1}{4}$ mile (400 m)

Week 3
Day 1: run 1 mile (1.5 km), sprint 2 × 220 yd (200 m), relax, jog $\frac{1}{4}$ mile (400 m)
Day 2: run 1$\frac{1}{2}$ miles (2.5 km), sprint 2 × 220 yd (200 m), relax, jog $\frac{1}{4}$ mile (200 m)
Day 3: run 2 miles (3 km), jog 1 mile (1.5 km), relax, jog $\frac{1}{4}$ mile (400 m)

Week 4
Day 1: run 1$\frac{1}{2}$ miles (2.5 km), sprint 3 × 220 yd (200 m), relax, jog $\frac{1}{4}$ mile (400 m)
Day 2: run 2 miles (3 km), sprint 3 × 220 yd (200 m), relax, jog $\frac{1}{4}$ mile (400 m)
Day 3: run 2$\frac{1}{2}$ miles (4 km), sprint 3 × 220 yd (200 m), relax, jog $\frac{1}{4}$ mile (400 m)

Week 5
Day 1: run 2$\frac{1}{2}$ miles (4 km), sprint 3 × 220 yd (200 m), relax, jog $\frac{1}{4}$ mile (400 m)
Day 2: run 3 miles (5 km), sprint 4 × 220 yd (200 m), relax, jog $\frac{1}{2}$ mile (800 m)
Day 3: run 3 miles (5 km), sprint 5 × 220 yd (200 m), relax, jog $\frac{1}{4}$ mile (400 m)

Week 6
Day 1: run 2$\frac{1}{2}$ miles (4 km), sprint 5 × 50 yd (50 m), relax, jog $\frac{1}{4}$ mile (400 m)
Day 2: run 2$\frac{1}{2}$ miles (4 km), sprint 6 × 50 yd (50 m), relax, jog $\frac{1}{4}$ mile (400 m)
Day 3: run 3 miles (5 km), sprint 7 × 50 yd (50 m), relax, jog $\frac{1}{4}$ mile (400 m)

Week 7
Day 1: run 3 miles (5 km), sprint 5 × 50 yd (50 m), relax, jog $\frac{1}{4}$ mile (400 m)
Day 2: run 3 miles (5 km), sprint 6 × 50 yd (50 m), relax, jog $\frac{1}{4}$ mile (400 m)
Day 3: run 3$\frac{1}{2}$ miles (5 km), sprint 7 × 50 yd (50 m), relax, jog $\frac{1}{4}$ mile (400 m)

Week 8
Day 1: run 3$\frac{1}{2}$ miles (5.5 km), sprint 5 × 50 yd (50 m), relax, jog $\frac{1}{4}$ mile (400 m)
Day 2: run 3$\frac{1}{2}$ miles (5.5 km), sprint 6 × 50 yd (50 m), relax, jog $\frac{1}{4}$ mile (400 m)
Day 3: run 4 miles (6.5 km), relax, jog $\frac{1}{4}$ mile (400 m)

Week 9
Day 1: run 3$\frac{1}{2}$ miles (5.5 km), sprint 5 × 50 yd (50 m), relax, jog $\frac{1}{4}$ mile (400 m)
Day 2: run 4 miles (6.5 km), sprint 5 × 50 yd (50 m), relax, jog $\frac{1}{4}$ mile (400 m)
Day 3: run 4$\frac{1}{2}$ miles (7 km), relax, jog $\frac{1}{4}$ mile (400 m)

Week 10
Day 1: run 4 miles (6.5 km), sprint 5 × 50 yd (50 m), relax, jog $\frac{1}{4}$ mile (400 m)
Day 2: run 3$\frac{1}{2}$ miles (5.5 km), sprint 6 × 50 yd (50 m), relax, jog $\frac{1}{4}$ mile (400 m)
Day 3: run 5 miles (8 km), relax, jog $\frac{1}{4}$ mile (400 m)

Pre-season practice

This is a schedule for a practice session I have run with my teams as part of their pre-season preparation.

As you can see we are at the teaching stage, with an emphasis on man-to-man defence and our motion offence. This session will last about two hours.

Stretch
● Led by the captain and lasting for 10–15 minutes

Fast break
● Three-man weave over the full court (5 minutes)
● 3-on-2 down to one end of the court then 2-on-1 back to the other end again (5 minutes)
● 5-on-0 with the secondary break, making sure that players 2 and 3 execute their cuts under the basket (10 minutes)

Man-to-man defence
● Mass shuffle (5 minutes)
● Zigs-zags (10 minutes)
● Guards practise denying the pass to the wing player; tall players practise fronting the post (10 minutes)
● Four-on-four shell drill, paying particular attention to blocking out (10 minutes)

Shooting
● Two-man jump shooting (10 minutes)
● Foul shots (5 minutes)
(Break for a drink)

Motion offence
● Players O1, O2 and O3 play three-on-three (10 minutes)
● Players O4 and O5 play five-on-five (10 minutes)
● Five-on-five controlled scrimmage (calling the fouls) over half court (10 minutes)

Scrimmage (15 minutes)
● Offence play fast break, secondary break and motion offence
● Defence play '5', our call sign for half-court man-to-man defence when we miss a field goal
● '55', which is the call sign for our full-court man-to-man defence when we score a field goal

Pre-season is an excellent time to spend on teaching or being taught

Game preparation practice

This is a typical practice to use the day before a game, to deal specifically with the tactics of opponents. It differs from a pre-season practice in that it is slightly shorter ($1-1\frac{1}{2}$ instead of 2 hours).

Stretch (10–15 minutes)

Press break offence (15 minutes)
● Versus no defence
● Versus 1-2-1-1 full court zone trap
● Versus full court man-to-man defence

Opposition plays
● Man-to-man defence (versus opponents' defence)
Five of your players, usually the second five (that is, not those who would normally start the game) run the 'dummy offence', which means they run the plays you expect your opponents to run in the next day's match.
    Their plays are
☐ 'Fist play' – which is a motion offence with three perimeter players and two inside players
☐ '1' play – a 1-4 alignment of the UCLA high post offence
☐ '5' play – setting double picks for players O2 and O3 to get free for jump shots from the wing
☐ Sideline out of bounds play
☐ Play a full speed scrimmage against all the offences (total 20 minutes)
    The first four drills are all 'walked through', that is, played at a walking pace, talking the players through the moves at the same time before running them at game speed in the scrimmage.
● Foul shots (10 minutes)
(Break for a drink)

Man-to-man offence half court (10 minutes)
Now we start to run through the offences we will use in the game against our opponents.
☐ '2' play – a 2-1-2 alignment of the UCLA high post offence
☐ '4' play – clearing out to make room for player O4. No defence against this drill
☐ High-low play – running a 1-3-1 alignment to isolate a tall man to get the ball on the right baseline. No defence
☐ 'Spread' – the four corners offence to pass the ball around and delay the play as long as possible within the time allowed on the shot clock allowance. Four players move to the corners of the baseline and sidelines and where the halfway line meets the sidelines. With the fifth player holding a central position they pass the ball around to leave their opponents little time to score after they regain possession. Teams use this at the end of a game to protect their lead.

Zone offence (10 minutes)
☐ 'Philly' – the Philadelphia 76ers overload offence
☐ '1 Go' – the 1-3-1 zone offence. No defence played in this drill
☐ '2 Go' – the 2-1-2 zone offence. No defence
☐ 'Box' – against the box-and-one defence

Foul shots (5 minutes)
Team talk and go home!

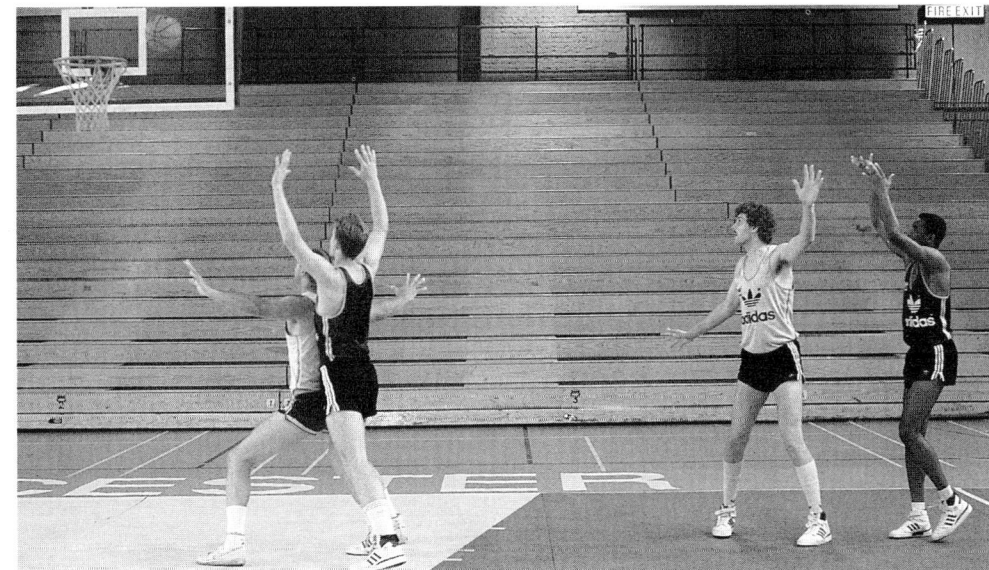

The shot has gone up from the player on the far right; now the defender closest to the basket boxes out his man to prevent the offensive rebound

BASKETBALL ASSESSMENT TEST

Station	Task	Personal score				
1	Right-hand lay-ups – timed					
2	Number of chest passes completed in one minute					
3	Number of bounce passes completed in one minute					
4	Round-the-world 4 times each way – timed					
5	Score 10 baskets from 6 different spots around the key – timed					
6	Dribble 10 yards (10 metres) forward then back – timed					
7	REST					
8	Left-hand lay-ups – timed					
9	Double bounce 2 balls at once 20 times – timed					
10	10 rebound and outlet passes – timed					
11	REST					
12	10 completed javelin passes – timed					
13	Defensive shuffle across foul line extended and back – timed					

Inevitably, you will need a lot of the time to practise on your own and just as inevitably your commitment and enthusiasm might occasionally fall short. A great way to motivate yourself for solitary practice is to keep a check of your progress and that is where this chart comes in.

Treat each vertical column as a particular day's practice session and enter either the amount of time it took you to complete the tasks or the number of exercises you completed in the allotted time. Use a pencil, lightly, so that you can re-use the chart.

Personal score

Personal score

RUNNING THE GAME

Basketball has come a long way since a Massachusetts College lecturer, Dr James Nai-smith, devised a game for his students involving throwing a ball into a basket suspended above the ground. But the object of the game is still the same, trying to score more points than your opponents. That job falls to the players, and each team can have five players on court at one time, out of a total of ten on each team (or 12 in some international tournaments). Substitutes 'from the bench' may be used to replace those on court when play stops.

Play starts with a jump ball when an official throws the ball up between two opponents and from then on points can be scored from anywhere on the floor by any player.

Points scored, fouls committed, time elapsed are all registered by the table of officials and transmitted to the scoreboard so that the crowd as well as players and coaches can quickly see the state of the game

Scoring

Players can score one, two, or three points for a shot: three if the shot is scored from beyond the long range arc drawn on the court floor, 22 ft (6.7 m) from the basket under international rules, 25 ft (8 m) in America's professional NBA and 19 ft 9 in (6 m) in America's college game. Two points are scored for field goals shot from within the arc and one point for each free throw, awarded after fouls or violations.

The only occasion when a basketball match can be left tied is where the result is an aggregate of the scores played over two matches, or 'two leg' games as they are called. So, if the first match is drawn the winners will be decided by the second leg match. As long as one team wins the

first match, a tie is allowed on the second game as one team will still be ahead on aggregate.

Each coach is allowed two time-outs in a half, each lasting one minute.

Timing

Although the NBA play their matches in four quarters of 12 minutes each, all other matches are played in two halves of 20 minutes, electronically-timed so that the clock stops each time the referee blows his whistle or when the table of officials signal a halt to play by operating their sounding device, usually a hooter, horn or buzzer. The game clock, which runs down to zero from 20 minutes at the beginning of each half, also stays stopped when a player is shooting free throws.

The influence of the clock in basketball is important, as time penalties are instrumental in making it such a fast game. When a team has to put the ball into play from the sideline or from under their basket, they have only five seconds to do so.

When the ball is in play they then have only 10 seconds to move the ball over the halfway line and a limited time in total to attempt a shot at their opponents' basket. This is 24 seconds in the NBA, 30 seconds in international rules (which means basketball played everywhere outside the USA) and 45 seconds in US colleges. Another time penalty stops players waiting under their opponent's basket, or 'cherry picking'. A player without the ball can stand in his opponent's lane for only three seconds.

It is these time penalties which help to make defence so exciting for crowds and players. A full-court press, for example, can be used to prevent a team moving the ball over the halfway line within the permitted 10 seconds. Once the team has advanced the ball over the halfway line, they are not allowed to take it back in their own half.

Officials

The officials comprise two on court, the referee and umpire, with equal responsibility and power, although the referee has the final say. They are assisted by table officials, comprising a scorer, time-keeper, 30-second operator and commissioner.

Fouls

Personal fouls result from holding or pushing or chopping an opponent's hands. Personal fouls are penalized by awarding free throws to the victim of the foul. If a player is fouled in the act of missing a shot he is allowed three attempts to score two points. If a player is fouled in the act of scoring a field basket, he is allowed one attempt to score a bonus shot.

Players are permitted to commit only a certain number of *personal fouls* (six in the NBA and five in international rules) before they have to leave the game, although a substitute can then be used.

Basketball legislates against unsportsmanlike play by awarding *technical fouls* for offences such as dissent, resulting in free throws for the opposition. This can also be applied for intentional fouling, as when a team are desperate to recover the ball in the final seconds of a close game.

Violations, such as an illegal dribble or failing to comply with one of the time penalties, are not personal fouls and are not penalized by free throws but simply by loss of possession.

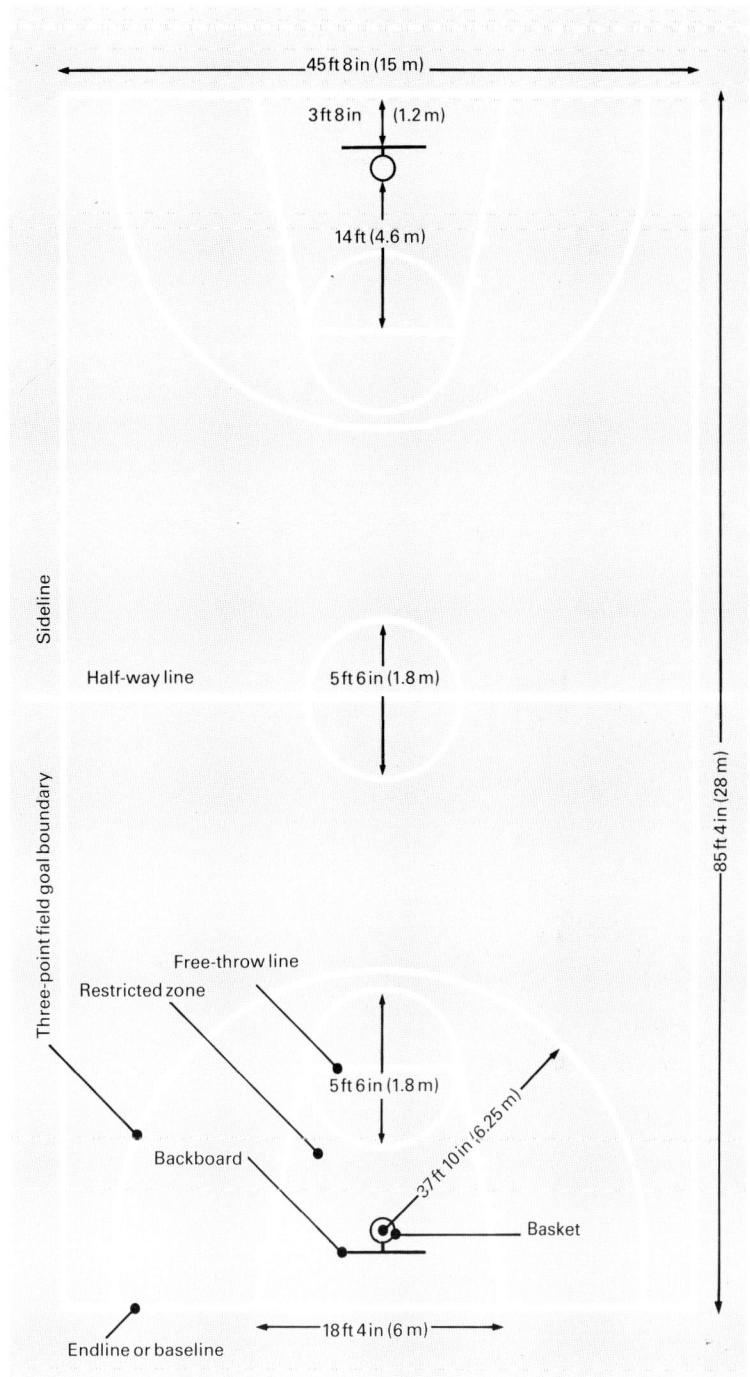

Dimensions of a basketball court

REFEREE'S SIGNALS

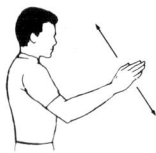

1 Time in
Chop with hand or finger

2 Official's time-out
Open palm

3 Charged time out
Form T, finger showing

4 Substitution
Crossed forearms

5 Jump ball
Thumbs up

6 Violation out of bounds
a Violations signal
b Direction of play

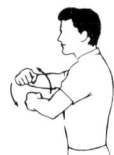

7 Travelling
Rotate fists

8 Illegal dribble
Patting motion

9 Three-second rule infraction
Fingers pointing to side

10 Cancel score, cancel play
Move arms across body

11 Personal foul
Clenched fist

12 Personal foul (no free throws)
Finger pointing to side line

13 Free-throws penalty
Fingers pointing to free-throw line, followed by signal of the number of free throws

14 Technical foul
Form T, palm showing

15 Double foul
Wave clenched fists

16 Intentional foul
Grasp wrist

17 Holding
Signal foul; grasp wrist

18 Charging
Clenched fist striking open palm

19 Pushing
Signal foul; imitate push

20 Illegal use of hands
Signal foul; strike wrist

21 Foul by team in control of ball
Both hands on hips

22 To designate offender
Hold up number of player

23 Two points (one finger-one point)
'Flag' from wrist

24 During free throws
Signal two throws

25 During free throws
Signal when no rebound can follow

26 Last free throw
Closed hand with pointed index finger

27 Three-point shot
Both arms in air

28 One-and-one free throws
Both arms in air with one finger pointing upwards

Referee with the ball at
the free-throw line

GLOSSARY

Assist A defence-splitting pass which leads directly to a basket being scored

Backboard The flat board, often transparent, on which the basket hangs. Usually called the 'boards', as in 'dominating the boards', which means taking most of the rebounds

Back court The half of the court containing a team's own basket

Bank shot Deflecting the shot off the backboard and into the net

Baseball pass One-handed overhead pass

Baseline The endline of the court, 3 ft 11 in (1.2 m) behind the backboard

Basket The name of the game! The target and the name for a score.

Blocking out or boxing out Taking up a position and stance to prevent an opponent from getting close to the basket.

Centre The tallest player in the team, a shot blocker and the leading rebounder who scores most of his or her points close to the basket

Charging foul When an offensive player charges into a stationary defensive player who has both feet firmly on the ground

Defence Individual and team moves which defend your basket. Abbreviated to 'D' as in 'playing tough D'

Denial defence Preventing players from receiving the pass by blocking the path between them and the passer

Double team see **Trap**

Double foul Simultaneous foul by opponents resulting in a jump ball to restart the game

Dunk One or two-handed shot thrusting the ball down through the ring. Also called a 'jam' or 'stuff'

Fakes Pretending to pass, shoot or dribble to force a defender off balance.

Fast break A quick attack, executed before the opposition take up their defensive positions

Field goal or basket Two or three-point shot scored from open play

Foul line Free-throw line

Free throw Awarded after fouls, shot unopposed from free-throw line and worth one point if successful

Front court The half of the court containing the basket which a team attacks

Getting open A player making himself free from a defender in order to receive a pass from a team-mate

High post Offensive position at the top of the lane around the foul line area

Hook shot One-handed overhead shot

Inbounds Putting the ball in to play

Inside Close to or under the basket

Jump ball Starts the match, second half or after certain violations when the official throws the ball up between two opponents

Jump shot One-handed shot released at the top of a jump

Jumper or 'J' Jump shot

Key Can be used to describe the Lane, the area marked out on the court floor from the baseline to the foul line

Lane The area marked out on the court floor from under the basket to the foul line

Lay-up One-handed shot delivered at the end of a run either directly into the basket or, usually, off the backboard

Low post The offensive position closest to the basket

Man-to-man defence Individual defenders guarding a specific opponent

Motion Offence where the players operate within a set of general rules

NBA National Basketball Association (USA)

Offence Individual and team moves which attack the opponents' basket

Off guard Usually taller than the point guard and a shooter

One-on-one One offensive player against one defender

Overtime Extra five-minute periods to break a tie at the end of normal time

Outlet pass The pass made by a player after he has taken a defensive rebound in order to get his team away on their offence

Outside Away from the basket and away from the lane area, which is drawn on the floor of the court under the basket

Passing lanes The areas closest to the body which it is most difficult for the defensive player to cover with his hands

Pick see **Screen**

Pivot Moving one foot while the other foot (the pivot foot) remains fixed to the floor

Point guard The ball-handler, play-maker or floor general of the team. An excellent passer. The point is the position in the middle of the offence. The player at 'point' need not necessarily have the ball

Power forward Tall and strong, a physical player who rebounds and scores close to the basket

Pressure defence Denying the pass and harassing the ball-handler. *Press* – playing pressure defence over the full length of the court, half-court or quarter-court

Rebound When the ball bounces from the backboard or the ring off a missed shot

Screen or pick Offensive player without the ball blocking the path of a defender who is chasing the dribbler (usually) or another offensive player without the ball

Small forward Often the most athletic team member, can shoot, drive, is fast and a good defender

Steal Taking the ball, legally, away from an opponent's hands

Strong side The side of the offence where the ball is held

Three-point shot A basket scored from outside the arc drawn on the court outside the lane area

Time-out Each coach may call two one-minute time-outs in each half and a further one in each period of overtime

Trap Two or more defenders trapping the offensive player with the ball

Travelling An illegal dribble caused when the player fails to bounce the ball correctly

Turnover Offensive team losing possession by passing to an opponent or by a dribbling or time violation, but *not* by committing a personal foul on an opponent

Violation An infringement which loses possession for the team with the ball

Weak side The side of the offence away from where the ball is being held

Zone defence Defenders guarding an area and any offensive player while he is in that area

ADDRESSES

Fédération Internationale de Basketball
BP 700607
Kistlerhofstrasse 16B
D-8000
Munich 70
Federal Republic of Germany

English Basket Ball Association
Calomax House
Lupton Avenue
Leeds LS9 6EE

Amateur Basketball Association of the USA
1750 East Bolder Street
Colorado Springs
Colorado 80909
USA

INDEX

*Figures in italics refer to
illustrations; figures in bold
refer to main entry*

Alcindor, Lew 46
Alford, Steve 27
'assist' 10, 18

'back door' 82, *82–83*
Barkley, Charles 40
baseline screen *93*
behind-the-back dribble
16, *16*
behind-the-back pass 22,
22
between-the-legs dribble
15, *15*
between-the-legs pass 22
Bird, Larry 18, 26, *40*, 83,
91, **92**
'block out' 44, *46*
Bogues, Tyrone 'Mugsy'
38
Bol, Manute 38, *63*
bounce pass 20, *20*
'box-and-one' 70, *71*
'box out' 44, *46*

'carrying' 13
'catch and go' 81
'catch and shoot' 81
centre 13
chest pass 19, *19, 25*
'clear out' 89
coach 8
controlled dribble 11, *11*
Cousy, Bob **18**, 43
Cowens, Dave 43
crossover dribble 12, *12*
crossover step 81, *81*

danger passes 22, *22, 23*
defence 13, **50–73**
defensive rebounding
42–43, *42, 43*
defensive stances 52–53,
52, 53
denial defence 56
diet 112
double picks 87, 94, 96
'double-teaming' *76*
dribbling 10–17, *10–16,
75*
work-outs 107
dunk shot 36, *37*

equipment 113

fakes 18, *80*, 81
fast break 14, 38, 39, 43,
98–99, *98–99*
follow-through 28
footwork 52, 74, 81, *81*
fouls 120
foul shot 34–35, *34*
free throw 34–35, *34*
full-court zone press
64–65, *64, 65*

game plan 73
'give and go' 84, 86
'going through' 58, *58*
guard pick 96
guarding 53

half-court zone press 66,
66
'high-low' 89, *89*
high-post play 39, 48, 94,
96
hook shot 35

individual moves 74–89,
74–89
'inside' 28

jab step 81
Jabbar, Kareem Abdul *29*,
35, **46**
Johnson, Magic 18, 30, *78*
Jones, K C 43
Jordan, Michael *25*, 36
jump hook shot 36, *36*
jump pass 22
jump shot *29*, 30–31, *30,
31*
jump stop 75
junk defences 70, 71, *70,
71*

'L cut' 82, *83*
lay-up shot 32–33, *32, 33*
low post 39, 48

Malone, Moses **40**, 41
man-to-man defence
50–61, *50–61*
man-to-man offence
90–103, *90–103*
match-up zone 69, *70*
motion offence 92–94

Naismith, James 8, 120

off guard 13
offence 13, **90–103**
offensive rebounding
44–45, *44, 45*
officials 120
Olajuwon, Akeem *29*
'one-on-one' 14
origins 8
outlet pass 21, *21, 42–43*,
43
'outside' 28
'over the top' 58, *58*
overhead pass 21, *21*

'pass and go behind' 85
'pass and screen' 86
passing 18–25, *19–23, 25*
work-out 108
pick 39, *39*
'pick and roll' 84, *84*, 87
pivoting 76, *76*, 81
point guard 13
possession 78
'post out' 83
power forward 13
press 57
pressure defence 57, 64
protected dribble 11, *11*
push shot 33

rebounding 26, **40–49**,
40–49
work-out 110
referee's signals *122*
reverse dunk shot *37*
reverse pivot 81
rocker step 81
Russell, Bill 43

Samson, Ralph *47*
scissors play 96
scoring 120
screen 39, *39*
secondary break 99–101,
100–101
'shake and bake' 14, *14*
shooting 26–39, *26–34,
36–39*
work-outs 108–9
signals, referee's *122*
Silas, Paul 45
'sky hook' 35
slides 66, *66*, 67, *67*, 69

Step by step basketball skills

small forward 13
speed dribble 11, *11*
spin dribble 13, *13*
'steal' 53
strong side 39
stutter step dribble 14, *14*
'switch' 58, *59*

team defence 58–61,
  58–61
Thomas, Isiah **10**, 18
three-point shot 27, *31*
timing 120

touch pass *22*
training 112–3, 114–9
trap 13, 64, *67*
'triangle and two' 71, *71*
triple threat position 78
turnover 53

UCLA high post offence
  96, *96*
underhand shot 33

'V cut' 82, *83*
violation 13

weak side 39
weave 86
Webb, Spud 36, **38**, *38*
Wilkins, Dominique 37
Williams, Buck 40
work-outs 104–112
Worthy, James *63*

zone defence 62–73,
  62–73
zone offence 102–3,
  102–3
zone press 64, 66, *72, 73*